Financial Strategies

for Real Estate Investing

2022

The Best Guide to learning how to contact investors and finance your real estate projects to retire with peace of mind and happiness

Table of Contents

Introduction

The idea of this book came to me in a flash, and I immediately decided to write it. Naturally, when you read it (the book), it may be a year from its writing, if not more, but the topic of real estate and making money on it will still be relevant. This is a kind of letter to the future for the reader, for my fans (or as I like to call them "adepts"), for my children, and of course, this book is for me. Yes, I love myself. I think there is a healthy share of selfishness in every person, but you need to be honest with yourself and others, admitting this.

This book is written in such a way that you can refer to any part of it, read it, and choose the strategy that interests you. Don't overload your brain. I can say one thing, all strategies are just a *bomb* because when I found out about them, from that moment I could no longer sleep. I, my wife, and my team implement some of them interchangeably and we are already seeing the results - we are already "blowing the tower". I think when you get acquainted with these strategies, then your "roof" will not remain in place.

Before you learn about these strategies, I would like to get acquainted and tell you a little about myself, what I am doing and where I am going. This will give you the understanding that I am just as common a person of flesh and blood as the rest of the world's population.

I want to make a reservation right away; I do not pretend to be a Real Estate Guru or anything else. I just love what I do, I love learning and teaching others. I like it when people change their thinking, become flexible, learn, apply knowledge. I don't like whiners, those who say that I won't succeed without even trying. I am struggling with this in myself, constantly eradicating all this rotten attitude that there is some kind of framework, setting, or something external that can interfere with me.

Okay, let's get to know each acquaintance.

I was born…. No, I'm not going to tell this, honestly. You can read this on my Facebook page or somewhere else. You are not reading this to find out where I was born, what I ate, drank, what clothes I wore. What's really important is that it's a business and a personal growth topic. In this book, I will talk a little about them, more about business and investing.

I'm Michael Steven - a best-selling author, entrepreneur, and investor. I have financed over $1 billion in real estate and have helped eliminate millions of dollars of debt. I have over 30 years of experience in finance and investment and have been teaching people how to get out and stay out of debt.

Helping you achieve financial freedom with not a lot of money matters deeply to me because what you're about to learn has made me more money than I could have ever imagined. I have helped thousands of people over the years to get out of debt, buy and sell properties, and guided them to their early retirement. I wrote this book because I want to give back to society and help people get an opportunity to benefit from my successes.

In my life, two incidents stuck in my memory, which greatly influenced me. And both of these moments affect me to this day, perhaps when I tell you about them, they will also affect you. Finally, something will click or close in your head, and the secrets of the universe will open before you and you will know universal love... just kidding, you won't know...

The first case, rather a thought, happened in childhood. Then I knew nothing about investing and other financial matters. My brother and I were walking across the field from home to the bus stop, and we started talking about our actions. At that time, our mother owned a good block of shares in the company in which she worked as a chief accountant, and thanks to dividends from these shares, we subsequently acquired an apartment and a bunch of other stuff we needed that we could have purchased at that time. The conversation turned to the fact that it would be better to buy more such shares and make money on them.

At that moment, the thought occurred to me that by buying stocks, I could save them, buy an apartment, and then another apartment and earn money like that, this was my first thought related to investing. I remember it clearly because at that moment it seemed to me just amazing. When I explained this to my brother, he told me that this was nonsense, that my mother had so many shares and, in general, we were just lucky.

Why am I telling you this? Wild ideas appear in our life that could have made us rich many years ago, but listening to the advice of people who do not understand this, incompetent people, we simply allow our dream, our soul, idea, thought to be torn apart by jackals. Words of people, such as you won't succeed, it's a stupid idea, it's too late or too early to do it, it's just luck, it's not for you, the market is overcrowded and other crap that is rubbed into us in childhood. I understand that you will not be able to drop all this now, but I urge you to *fight*. Always fight these thoughts, these words of other people, do not let jackals torment and tear down your ideas, dreams, and plans. Hold on to the last, and you will see how these people shut up and begin to envy you because in their eyes you are doing the impossible.

The second case was much more revealing, deeper emotionally, and closer to the topic about which this book is written. There are two people and one apartment in this story. Me, my mom, and the apartment.

When we moved to Colorado, my mother had a fixed idea that she needed to buy an apartment, this idea began to dominate her so much that it seemed she lived only for it. As I said above, where we came from, we already had an apartment, it was a three-room apartment and a large house with a garage for 2 cars in a good quiet location. To have more understanding, I will explain the situation, imagine... Here you live, you have money, a prestigious, profitable job, you are respected, people come to you for advice, they listen to you. You have a big apartment, a big house, and a big friendly family. It so happens that you have to move to another state. The price for which we could sell an apartment at that time was $ 350,000, the market then fell. I had to move to a new place where there are no connections, no acquaintances, no friends, no family, no real estate, and no status. Well, we sold the house a little later for about $600,000.

And so, continue to imagine the situation…. Life was sweet and here in Colorado, the price for a one-room apartment in the Colorado region at that time was on average $2,000,000!!! Can you imagine our *shock*? And then we felt it, especially my mother, a person who was used to living in abundance, either in the large apartment living room or living and relaxing in her bedroom house.

What are we doing? At that time, with travel, food, and many other expenses, we already had time to spend a certain amount of money, and we had very little of it left. We had relatives on my father's side and through my second cousin, my mother managed to borrow $800,000 from a rich friend.

And guess what we were able to buy ourselves? With this money, we bought a three-room apartment, a two-story old house in a town 50 km from the Colorado city center.

Mom then started working two, then three, then four extra jobs to pay back the loan... and it was terrible. How to explain that feeling when you see how a person burns out, on the one hand, she had a goal that she had been pursuing for more than one year, on the other hand, she simply killed her body, and instead of growing, she was looking for a solution in the fact that I have to get one more job. Then she no longer worked in a cool position in the accounting department, her eyesight was fading, she helped other accountants during the day, at lunchtime she went to the police station and washed the floors there, then in the evening she washed the floors in a warehouse and worked part-time by consulting on various issues.

Then something happened.

A person who had lived for many years with the idea of buying an apartment fully paid for, giving it his health, time, energy, emotions, having finally received this result, just started to get sick. Mom was diagnosed with cancer. I was the first to find out about this diagnosis from the doctor. None of my relatives wanted to take on the responsibility to talk to my mother about it, so I took it. I told her that she was sick with cancer and she had about six months to live since this was a malignant tumor. She was sick, and the reason for this was her lifestyle. Her quick snacks, constant stress, nervousness over all sorts of little things, constant work. For what?

You see, my mother, as they say about such people, was punchy, she is a "terminator". If she set a goal, then she went for it until she reached it. The only thing that she lacked was the knowledge of how to do so to get it quickly, without undermining her health, with nervous breakdowns and humiliating work for her.

I want to convey to you one idea, the fact is that you can be like my mother, kill yourself at two, three, four jobs and work like a terminator, going towards the goal to buy yourself a house, an apartment or a car, or you can raise your head and understand what the better options are for achieving your goal. There are a lot of options, the strategies which I shall describe here in this book. You can achieve your goal without harming your health, without sacrificing your time, without nervous breakdowns, and even without money. First, understand how it works, spend your time on financial literacy, not TV. Choose what you like in this book and, after reading about this strategy, start implementing it.

If my mom had been made aware of these strategies at the time I got to know them, I think she would still be alive, and we would have had a lot more properties, but this is also a lesson, not only for me, this lesson is also for you...

The topic of real estate is very profitable and interesting if you really get excited about it and learn how to make money using three factors: a) someone else's hands; b) other people's money; c) someone else's time; then your life will change dramatically.

D. Trump said about real estate: "It is tangible, durable, and beautiful. From my point of view, she is even artistic. I just love real estate." With these words of his, which I also subscribe to, we will begin to analyse the best strategies for investing in real estate without investing your own money. Go!

Chapter One: Basics of Real Estate Investing

Each new investor must have a solid understanding of investment fundamentals. While building a solid foundation is absolutely necessary to create financial stability, wealth, or attain retirement goals, building a good foundation in real estate investing will provide the same benefits.

When it comes to investments, while there are certain shared traits between real estate investing and more traditional ways like the stock market, mutual funds, or municipal bonds, there are also a significant number of variances. While you may be well acquainted with phrases such as return on investment (ROI), yield, or dividends, it's still possible to feel frightened when you're presented with unfamiliar phrases like net operating income, cap rate, or pro forma.

Let's begin by taking some time to review some real estate investment essentials, which will help you get a firm footing as you enter the world of real estate investing.

Why do people invest in the first place?

By putting money into an investment account, you can create or supplement your income, which can be utilized to expand your nest, raise your savings account, and build financial security far into retirement.

While Social Security is helpful for many individuals, many others won't have enough income to survive through retirement or may not have Social Security in its current form for the long term. In that case, you may need to prepare for the possibility of an additional source of income in the future, and this could help you financially in retirement. To begin saving money and building that nest, just set aside a little each pay period and earn interest on the difference. The faster your money increases, the larger the return you'll receive.

A large percentage of investors have portfolios that comprise various investments such as stocks, bonds, and real estate, and some just invest in stocks and bonds. Although the big discussion over which investment is better, which is real estate, is subject to strong opinions, no one can deny that real estate may be a valuable asset to an investment portfolio, and the fact that real estate:

- can provide consistent passive income
- has the potential to appreciate or increase in value over time
- provides you with the ability to use as debt surety to raise your net purchasing power and return on investment

It also has the ability to generate substantial returns, ranging from 8 to 15 percent.

While investing in any sort of asset class has risk, most of the risk associated with real estate investing may be minimized by a careful pre-investment due diligence process. Now, let's have a look at the many options for investing in real estate.

Investing strategies for real estate

With regard to the topic of passive versus active investment, you can invest in real estate passively, which means you are a passive participant and are not responsible for managing the property or investment yourself; or actively, in which you are an active participant and are responsible for acquiring, managing, and disposing of the property.

Passive Real Estate Investing

Passive investments are better suited for people who are willing to devote less time to their investments, as they do not demand the same amount of daily involvement. In general, active investments tend to have greater rates of return. Prior to investing in real estate, take the time to assess your schedule to determine how much time you will devote to your real estate investment endeavors. Determine the investment type you're most comfortable with to fit your available time and desire for engagement.

Passive investments generate an income stream termed cash flow, which is often provided in the form of rental income or dividends. Income in the form of passive sources, such as interest, dividends, and capital gains, is taxed differently than ordinary income, and many people prefer to earn this type of income.

It is not uncommon for investors who have begun investing to desire to branch out of the stock market and diversify their portfolios by investing in real estate. While it may seem difficult to engage in real estate, there are still other options to participate in real estate through REITs and ETFs.

REITs

A Real Estate Investment Trust (REIT) is a company whose shares have a specific designation, and they are bought and owned by a collection of investors who each pool together a certain amount of money. That money is returned to investors in the form of a dividend that pays at least 75% or more of all profits made. REITs can be publicly listed or privately traded, and traditionally they have had a great track record.

Investing in REITs is a simple matter. It only requires purchasing shares from a brokerage account for a few hundred dollars. While there are two basic categories for REITs, the general types of REITs include equity REITs and mortgage REITs, nevertheless, it is possible to find CRE firms that serve a different kind of commercial real estate (CRE). Compared to investing in stocks, investing in REITs is quite simple and allows even those who have minimal financial resources to start investing in real estate.

ETFs

An Exchange-Traded Fund (ETF fund) works in a similar manner to a mutual fund, but instead of simply investing in mutual funds, the fund invests in real estate-related commodities like REITs. The fund manager selects individual REITs to invest in, which gives investors who acquire shares in the real estate ETF the ability to diversify their portfolio holdings across several different CRE sectors and with several different REITs.

If you have a brokerage account, you may buy a real estate ETF for as little as a few hundred dollars, making this a good entry investment.

Crowdfunding

Investors that are looking to invest in real estate can look into participating in a crowdfunding platform that connects a sponsor, the active partner in the business, with funds from several investors. A highly desirable investment opportunity is professionally handled by the sponsor and the sponsor's staff, who guarantee an investor an above-average return over a certain length of time. When an investor invests in a crowdfunding venture, he may not be able to access his cash for some time. That means he'll have to pay a penalty to get his money back. While it is possible to earn a good return by utilizing crowdfunding as a passive investment, it does come with risk.

Real estate that is for rental purposes

In rental real estate, monthly rent is collected and earnings are produced as a result. Unlike in a job where you get paid for the hours you work, a landlord receives monthly cash flow, even though he or she does not have to spend the same amount of hours to do so. The rental income is constant. Although your income source could potentially be a stable one in retirement, you need to keep an eye on the rental payments if you hope to continue to generate stable cash flow in the long term.

If you're looking to rent a residential property, like a single-family home, condo, or triplex, you can do so or you can choose to rent a commercial property, such as an office, industrial building, retail center, or apartment complex.

The IRS believes rental revenue is passive, yet an investor is still involved because he or she must participate in lease activities to obtain the financial benefits of owning the property. Investors have a significant obligation since they must research, monitor, and manage every investment possibility; moreover, they must have title and ownership for the property, which includes paying for taxes and insurance, as well as making necessary maintenance and improvements.

In terms of management, the more passive or active a rental property is, the more important it is. If you employ a third-party management organization to undertake continuing management for you, they will take care of it. Alternatively, you can take care of it yourself. When it comes to rental properties, the priChloe consideration is the amount of work required. What factors influence your investment decisions is a complex question, which can only be answered after you have investigated a number of potential investment opportunities.

Residential real estate is a popular beginning point for new investors because of the reduced upfront costs making it an easier entry point. In many circumstances, getting a mortgage for a $100,000 single-family residence is easier than receiving a commercial loan for a $1,000,000 commercial building. Commercial properties are assessed differently than residential properties, which means it's crucial to be able to differentiate between various forms of rental real estate in order to identify which investment plan is the best fit for you.

High-return private equity fund

A private equity fund collects capital from a number of investors and invests that money in real estate assets. The management and their staff are responsible for allocating and managing investments, giving investors a preferred return or dividend on a monthly or quarterly basis. Commercial real estate investments may be made in privately-held private equity funds, which invest in commercial real estate, residential real estate, and real estate debt like performing or non-performing mortgage notes.

For a length of time set by the private equity fund, investment funds deposited in that fund are illiquid, which means the investor is unable to get his or her money out of the fund without incurring a penalty. Security Exchange Commission (SEC) rules require private equity funds to pool their money according to certain guidelines and are not available to the general public.

The practice of drawing mortgage notes

You are not actually investing in real estate when you invest in a mortgage note. Instead, you are investing in the debt that backs up the property.

Just as a bank will advance funds to acquire a property, an individual might advance funds to acquire a home. To meet a financial obligation, a property buyer signs a note and mortgage guaranteeing to repay the debt and makes a monthly payment to the lender, whose proceeds serve as both the principal and interest payment.

In this case, the investor earns passive income in the form of cash flow as long as the borrower is making regular payments.

Passive Real Estate Investing

Active real estate investments involve active participation throughout the entirety of the investment. An important difference to bear in mind is that real estate investment often acts like a business, where only earnings are received if you are actively working on the property. Rental real estate is classified as passive because it depends on the management, but it can be deemed an active real estate investment if the landlord chooses to focus on tenant improvements.

Fix and flip

With a fix-and-flip investment, you purchase a property, make modifications to boost its value, and then sell the property. The goal of this strategy is to profit from the property by selling it. The investor needs to have active management skills to successfully flip a house. They will also have to deal with negotiating a cheap purchase price for a property, doing the repairs themselves, or supervising and managing the contractors to complete the work. Fix-and-flips can be a good method to make a huge amount of money in a short length of time, but they are taxed at the upper end of the tax bracket because it is a short-term capital gain.

Wholesaling

Buying in bulk (or wholesaling) is the act of performing the necessary research and groundwork to uncover an unlisted or undervalued opportunity, negotiating a very cheap purchase price, and then assigning that contract to a wholesaler (buyer) at a somewhat higher price. The wholesaler makes a fee from the difference between the agreement between the seller and the buyer, and the agreement between the buyer and the seller. When it comes to starting as an active real estate investor, wholesaling is an easy way to get started because you just need a little amount of money. While you must put in a lot of time, it is not impossible. The only way to earn cash is to be a wholesaler if you have a sales opportunity pending.

Person-to-person short-term rentals

In contrast to long-term rentals, which are also referred to as holiday rentals, short-term rentals, such as holiday rentals, are usually leased for a nightly or weekly period. An increasingly popular short-term renting option is short-term rental services like VRBO and Airbnb, which enable property owners to rent out a piece of their home or the full house. When a property is utilized in a short-term rental manner, it should be provided and maintained by the property owner, including checking in and out the tenants and cleaning the property at the end of their stay.

When it comes to short-term rentals, it can be more profitable than long-term rentals, but on the other hand, it's more inconsistent. The rate of vacancy is related to where the property is located and the demand for vacation or short-term rentals in the area. During seasons of high vacancy, rental property owners can make large profits, while during periods of high occupancy, owners must devote considerable time to operations. Before deciding to rent space in your home or to buy a vacation rental, make sure you know the relevant local regulations and rules so you know if you may legally offer a short-term rental in your city or county. Many towns have regulations or license requirements that are unique to them.

Real estate investments and tax deductions

Because real estate is taxed differently based on the type of property you own, it is important to evaluate your options for buying and selling property before investing in real estate. A REIT's dividends are taxed differently than those of regular stock dividends. Additionally, rental real estate is taxed differently than a fix-and-flip investment strategy would be. If you invest in real estate tax-free or tax-deferred, you can earn additional income. You should understand how your property investment(s) will influence your taxes, depending on where you live, before purchasing your first piece of real estate.

To take the plunge, or not?

Investing is always risky, even though there are some assurances. No matter where you place your money, whether, with a financial advisor, the S&P 500, or in real estate, your investments will be relatively safe. However, there is always the possibility that you could lose your money or get a return that is less than what you planned. With asset allocation, you may diversify your portfolio across multiple real estate methods, but it's still possible to take risks with investments. Before you make any investment in real estate, you should assess your risk tolerance and continue to complete your due diligence on numerous investment options, so you can identify which real estate investment strategy is suitable for you.

Remember though, the wealthiest people in the world have earned their fortunes in numerous ways, but one common factor connects many of them: they have utilized real estate as a critical component of their investing plan. When it comes to all the ways the ultra-rich made their fortunes, real estate performed 3-to-1 better than all the others.

Do you want to also invest like the wealthiest people in the world? If so, keep reading to find out the best possible way(s) to do so.

In summary...

- Each new investor must have a solid understanding of investment fundamentals.
- Passive investments are better suited for people who are willing to devote less time to their investments, as they do not demand the same amount of daily involvement.
- In general, active investments tend to have greater rates of return.
- When it comes to short-term rentals, it can be more profitable than long-term rentals, but on the other hand, it's more inconsistent.

Chapter Two: Finding the Perfect Real Estate Investment Niche

Investing in real estate may be very complex. However, one of the most widely accepted pieces of advice to investors of all ages is to find a specialized niche in the real estate market. For example, perhaps you are asking what exactly a real estate niche is. To find real estate niches, I've developed a guide. In this chapter, you'll see the various sorts of niches available to investors, the factors you'll need to take into consideration when picking a niche, and what it means to be a successful investor.

Rental of houses remains the most popular real estate investment niche. Rents continue to rise in the single-family home rental industry, with many real estate markets showing increases of 3-5% or more. And for many years, the housing stock has not kept up with demand. Such conditions can offer excellent potential for investors who own real estate with rental yields.

For people with an interest in real estate, what is a real estate niche?

A niche can also be a term that means a specialized area of expertise. Often, real estate investors seek to focus their investments in a particular location, which they do to limit their losses. This is particularly true for investors who are new to the market and have not yet had the opportunity to diversify their portfolios. It is, nevertheless, the case that even the most seasoned investors will have at least one section of the real estate sector they love.

While the definition of a real estate investing niche differs from that of a real estate investment strategy, both have similarities. To put it another way, while a real estate investment strategy is the way you earn money in real estate, a niche is the particular investment vehicle where you use that strategy.

A good idea for someone who wishes to rent out residential real estate properties to long-term renters would be to implement a buy-and-hold strategy in real estate and focus on renting single-family houses. At the same time, someone who pursues a fix-and-flip approach may target houses located in rising communities with financial difficulties.

Real estate has different niches

The real estate market has several distinct options for you to choose from. I've done the hard work for you and listed many of the various possibilities that I've discovered. This is not a comprehensive list, but it should give you some ideas to consider while searching for new things to get into.

1. Property-related niches

The other specialty you might think of as a real estate investor is specializing in a certain property type. Among the most popular investment property kinds are:

- Dwellings occupied by a single family
- Multifamily dwellings, such as duplexes, triplexes, and quadplexes
- Apartments and condominiums
- Duplexes
- Land in its natural state

2. Commercial real estate specialization

While this may seem peculiar, the distinction is important since it indicates the type of person that lives in residential and commercial properties. In contrast to industrial real estate, commercial real estate has some unique features. Beginners should generally avoid it. However, my other book goes over the strategy of investing in commercial real estate in great detail. If you're interested in investing in commercial real estate, there are a variety of options for you to select from:

- Space for retail
- Office space
- Industrial space
- Self-storage facility
- Industrial-allocation land
- Real estate investment trusts (REITs) (EFTs)

In either of the two options above, you can choose to focus on a specific section of the country, town, or city. However, if your entire portfolio is invested in a single real estate market, and there is a downturn, it could take some time for your assets to return to their previous value.

Finding the perfect niche is a necessary next step once you have a better grasp of the numerous real estate niches. By simplifying the process, I have reduced it into several simple steps:

1. Real estate investment niches can not be determined until an investment goal is set. You will ultimately select how you wish to invest based on your investment objectives.
2. The next stage in choosing an available and achievable real estate investment fund is to settle on an investment plan. Many factors influence investing decisions, but thinking about the possibilities in your market helps you zero in on opportunities.
3. To prepare a solid business plan for establishing a real estate firm, be sure to perform extensive research. Before deciding on a specialization, you should explore all of your possibilities. It is always a good idea to review the list of specialties above, to make sure nothing has changed. Speaking with an expert in the real estate investing profession in your area is a great way to gain further guidance.

Weighing the pros and cons

Now it's time to investigate everything in each niche so that you can become better acquainted with everything out there. The real estate market has unique advantages and disadvantages for every group.

While this may not be exactly true, purchasing luxury real estate almost always results in a higher return. In contrast, the up-front cost is higher. As a result, you will not be able to transact the same volume of transactions at a reduced pricing range.

Once you've decided how much you're willing to invest, you must then determine whether or not you're willing to accept the accompanying risks and benefits. As a result, choose your course of action. If you have thoroughly investigated all of your options, you will have all the knowledge you need to decide which market sector is right for you.

Additionally, remember: a real estate niche is not "set in stone".

Choosing a career you loathe doesn't have to be an option. It's perfectly fine if you'd like to experiment with a different one. You might find a second place to invest if your investment portfolio diversifies.

All in all, to sum it up, here are the takeaways. Looking into a specific area of real estate can help you form a path for your future investments. Take this subject seriously, and think it through carefully.

In summary…

- Rental of houses remains the most popular real estate investment niche.
- Rents continue to rise in the single-family home rental industry, with many real estate markets showing increases of 3-5% or more.

Chapter Three: Finding Good Deals on Properties

You may be looking to invest in real estate for a variety of reasons: you may want to invest to pursue your long-term goals, or you may be just starting out and trying to build your portfolio. Regardless of your ambitions, starting out will require finding the best offers in your neighborhood. If you can accomplish it, you're in a great position for success today and in the future.

When it comes to possibilities, you should look for them, rather than wait for them to find you. You can locate real estate investment opportunities by being hard-working and knowledgeable. It's not a game of chance. If you're able to keep up, you can always win.

While using a real estate agent to assist you to identify properties for sale may be a good idea, it might not be the ideal way to go about it. Or are there better deals being bought and sold by those who are directly involved in the real estate industry, and we don't know about them? Yes, and there is a solution.

So, begin by considering two of the best techniques for latching on to profitable opportunities in your local area.

Gaining a monetary profit through driving

When it comes to investing, don't sit on your hands waiting for something to drop in your lap. Instead, take to the streets and search for houses in neighborhoods of interest. "Driving for dollars" is our term for this tactic. While you're traveling, you should keep your eyes peeled for two different kinds of properties, FSBOs and distressed or abandoned properties. Let's talk about each one of these.

1. FSBOs (For Sale By Owner)

These properties that are listed by owners without a real estate agent, or as "for sale by owner" (FSBO), comprise a minor component of the market but are routinely disregarded by larger players. You have the freedom to make your own decisions on what to do next. It's that simple.

All you have to do is hop in your car, drive around your area, or investment zone, and search for opportunities. Be it for sale by the owner, you are bound to see an FSBO homemade sign in nearly every market. This indicates that a property owner is interested in selling, but hasn't yet been listed by a real estate agency.

One way to do this is to take a photograph, note down the phone number, or approach the house and knock on the door. You should do everything in your power to lock down these discounts. In addition to that, you'll also avoid paying an agent's fee because you're most likely able to negotiate a fair bargain.

2. Properties in distressed or abandoned condition

When you notice homes that seem in disrepair or are vacant, pay attention. Disheveled properties have their appearance and definition in common with distress properties, meaning that both properties have a serious need for maintenance or are forsaken or abandoned. Generally, as the amount of work a property requires increases, the leverage you have to negotiate higher reductions increases.

The following are a few good identifiers that indicate a property has been abandoned or is in a state of distress:

- A mailbox that is overflowing with letters
- An abandoned building site with a code violation label
- Boarded up windows or doors; or shattered windows or doors
- There is no meter box, or the master switch is off
- Long, uncut grass and shrubbery
- A roll of tarp on the roof
- A lot of garbage, junk, or waste in front of the house

In most cases, a residence will appear unkempt or abandoned since there is usually a good reason. For example, in the case of the seller, if he is now in foreclosure, what is he supposed to do next? It's possible that they took care of the house for years, and now they can't because of their poor financial situation. No matter how difficult the selling environment is, you're almost certain to have seen a motivated seller. Stop other investors from getting there first, and you could have an excellent investment on your hands.

You may find a property that appears to be abandoned or in distress but with no seller information or anyone in the house. In this case, write down the address of the property. You must note the street address and the number of houses opposite and adjacent to it.

With that in mind, have your property search done on Google or Zillow.com so you can begin investigating the matter. Zillow.com will deliver crucial information, like the name of the property owner, the number of bedrooms and bathrooms, the square footage, whether or not it's in foreclosure or pre-foreclosure, and their contact information. Or you could ask the neighbors of the property in a nice manner. This usually saves time and yields amazing results if done calmly and politely.

Once you've acquired a thorough understanding of the property, you will be able to come up with a creative strategy to take it. A simple example would be if a property was in foreclosure. You may be allowed to contact the bank to make an offer before it is put up for auction.

If the home is physically distressed and unkempt, you will first attempt to locate the owners. Once you find them, you will attempt to get in touch with them by SMS and phone until you get through to them and can make an offer. You may be able to get the owner's phone number using whitepages.com, which will make searching much easier. To roughly estimate, a basic rule of thumb is to call three times, and no more so as not to agitate the seller and lose out on the future deal.

In addition, you may wish to use email to contact them. Convey that you're a real estate investor by writing a straightforward letter describing your buying strategy: that you acquire houses outright, for cash. You should also give step-by-step instructions on how to proceed if they are interested in selling. Include your website or a phone number to call, so others can contact you. If you have not yet delivered the letter, be sure to place it in the mailbox or at the front door.

Going a step further, you could knock on the door and see if anyone is home. Do not be scared to introduce yourself to the homeowner and explain what you do if you are given an answer.

"Hello, I'm a local real estate investor in the region, and I'm interested in purchasing several houses on this street. Do you have your home for sale? Do you know of anyone else in the neighborhood who has their property for sale?"

Lest we forget, you're making a big jump with this. Some doors will get slammed in your face, will they not? Yes, of course. However, if you can weather the storm, you are almost certain to receive many valuable "yeses". And this is always good news.

The bottom line is this strategy can result in great prices, even if the homeowners are not actively wanting to sell.

Word-of-mouth marketing

Acquiring real estate can also be done with word-of-mouth marketing. Word-of-mouth is one of the best techniques for locating outstanding real estate offers. Make everyone aware of your intentions. It's always a good idea to approach your friends, relatives, neighbors, and colleagues, and let them know that you're seeking to acquire an investment property or two.

It is important to note that real estate investing is *not* a lonely sport. There is someone out there who is thinking about selling their home, is ready to sell, or is in a jam and desperately wants to get out. If you can be the solution to their problem, if you can get a property off their hands, there's a good possibility you can pick up an incredible property for a great price.

Word of mouth is fantastic since you have the opportunity to conduct transactions with sellers before they list their properties for sale.

Say, for example, that Uncle Peter found out that the next-door neighbor Chloe had accepted a new promotion and would be moving to another state. It will be critical that she rapidly sells her home. It is clear Uncle Peter knows you need properties, so he offers Chloe your contact information.

Chloe tells you that she has to relocate in a hurry, and she asks you to keep her deposit secure. With the information you provide to Chloe, she knows you are a real estate investor who purchases houses with cash and closes quickly (which brings a smile to Chloe's face).

Now you see what just happened, don't you? It's beginning to look like there might be a deal in the works.

You can also chat with other individuals in your region who are well-informed about the areas and neighborhoods in which you live. It might be anyone, whether it's a long-term resident, the mailman, or someone who makes regular deliveries in the region. Stay-at-home moms who even take their babies on daily walks could also prove invaluable.

They can serve as your eyes and ears, always keeping an eye out for any indicators of potential—a few rogue strands of grass and a stack of papers heralding an abandoned house, an FSBO sign that appeared overnight, or a hint of local conversation which indicates that the neighbor is moving to Florida.

Have a direct relationship with them. Let them know that you're on the quest for amazing offers and that you have what you're searching for in mind. These guys will let you know when there are great offers on the horizon.

Putting it all together

Tick the box of everyone you know, and then plant the seed. Make a special effort to search your neighborhood for FSBOs and distressed properties to look for listings "this afternoon". As your concentration and knowledge of your subject increases, you have a better chance of outbidding others and securing a decent deal before everyone else gets a chance.

Picking up these great deals is the first step in creating your investment portfolio and your long-term riches. Finally, it is time to get out there and start looking for your first or next amazing investment property.

In summary…

- Tick the box of everyone you know, and then plant the seed.
- As your concentration and knowledge of your subject increases, you have a better chance of outbidding others and securing a decent deal

before everyone else gets a chance.

Chapter Four: Top Features of a Profitable Rental Property

Rental investments can be exciting and very rewarding if you make the right choices. But beyond the income and the gratification of your ego, investing in real estate can be daunting for a first-time investor.

Too many questions, too many doubts, too many fears. This is why it is important to do in-depth research before embarking on the adventure, to know all the advantages and disadvantages of your real estate rental investment.

Here are the most important points to consider when looking for profitable real estate to invest in:

1. **Location, Location, Location**

It is a habit of seasoned investors to think of the location as golden.

The neighborhood in which you buy your apartment, building, or house will determine the types of tenants you attract, your rent, and your occupancy rate. The location not only makes it possible to rent to many tenants but also to plan for different types of rentals with the rental returns that go with it. If you're buying near a university, there's a good chance that students will dominate your potential rental market, and you might have a hard time filling your units when the university is on break.

A shared tenancy is also an option to consider in these circumstances and makes it possible to increase the rents.

2. **Property tax**

Property tax varies a lot depending on the city and region you're investing in, and you need to know how much you're going to pay. You also need to know the dynamics of property tax in the area you want. High property taxes are not always a bad thing, but they do not indicate the quality of life in a particular neighborhood or street. Some unattractive places still have a high property tax though. You can get information from the town planning department of your municipality or location of choice.

Make sure you find out if property tax increases are likely in the near future. The consultation with neighbors is essential in this sense. Increases in property taxes are likely in two situations:

1. If taxes have not or little increased for years,
2. If the property tax increases regularly each year by a percentage higher than inflation.

A city in financial difficulty can raise taxes well beyond what a landlord can reasonably charge for rent.

3. Schools / Colleges / High schools

Consider the quality of local schools if you are renting apartments with more than one bedroom for couples with children. Also, while you are mostly concerned with monthly rents, the overall value of your rental investment kicks in when you do end up selling it.

If there are no good schools nearby, it can affect the value of your investment and limit the potential for capital gain.

4. Security

No one wants to live next to a crime and delinquency hotspot. The municipal police must have accurate statistics on crime in the neighborhoods in which you want to invest. Exchange, discuss, build relationships with the police. Check the rates of vandalism, serious crimes, and minor misdemeanors, and be sure to note whether criminal activity is increasing or decreasing. You can also find out about the frequency of police presence in your neighborhood with a neighborhood survey.

Another way to detect a problem in the neighborhood is to follow the evolution of real estate prices in the area over several years. If they are lower than in the rest of the city and keep going down…run away.

5. Labor market

Places offering more and more employment opportunities attract more tenants. It makes sense, but you still have to do some research. To find out how a specific region has the availability of jobs, consult the website of the National Institute of Statistics.

If you see an advertisement about setting up a large company in the area, you can be sure that workers looking for a place to live will flock there.

This can lead to higher or lower house prices, and rents, depending on the type of business involved. You can assume though that if a big business moves to a city, tenants will too.

Conversely, if employment in a locality is essentially based on a single large company, your rental investment is likely to be depreciated if it moves.

6. Leisure and entertainment possibilities

Take a tour of the neighborhood where you are considering a rental investment and discover all the elements of a pleasant living environment that attracts tenants, such as:

- parks
- restaurants
- sports halls
- cinemas
- public transport
- tourist attractions

The town hall or tourist office may have promotional materials that can give you an idea of where the best balance is between public infrastructure and residential areas.

7. Future development / Potential for Plus Value

The town planning department will have information on developments or projects and equipment that are to come into the area. If there is a lot of construction going on, this is probably a good growing area. Watch out for new buildings that could lower the price of surrounding properties. Also, note that many additional units could compete with your rental investment.

Conversely, infrastructure such as a tramway or a motorway entrance is a very positive signal for the future development of the value of your property.

8. Number of advertisements and the vacancy rate

If a neighborhood has an unusually high number of listings, it may signal that it is a neighborhood in decline. Unfortunately, high vacancy rates force landlords to lower rents to attract tenants. A low vacancy rate allows landlords to increase rents.

This is the logic of supply and demand, what we call Yield Management.

9. Average rents

The rental income will be your source of income, so you need to know the minimum average rent of the neighborhood or the street in which you invest.

Don't smile, this is a very common mistake with seasoned investors who tend to trust their lucky stars too much rather than the numbers. Make sure that your rental investment can easily generate enough monthly rent to cover your:

- mortgage
- local taxes
- other current charges

Do enough research on the region to be able to assess how it will evolve over the next five years.

If you can afford to buy a property in the area today, but taxes were to rise, a property that is affordable today could lead you to bankruptcy later. You should therefore always consider an unfavorable scenario in your market research, in order to be prepared for any unfavorable development.

10.   Natural disasters

Insurance is another expense that you will need to subtract from your rents, so you need to know how much it will cost you. And above all, never cut back on insurance.

Insurance always costs more and more every day, but it saves your life in the event of a hard blow, like water or fire damage.

If a city is prone to landslides, thunderstorms, hurricanes, tornadoes, or floods, the costs of good insurance can however significantly erode your rental income.

We experienced an earthquake and some houses on the edge of the municipality have never been covered by insurance because the municipality as a whole had too few claims while the houses concerned were very close to the epicenter!

Obtaining reliable information

To better invest your money in "stone", it is essential to research all the necessary information on your investment. The official sources are interesting, and I have shown you ten tips above to help you go further (or stop a future deal) if necessary. But you'll have to talk to the neighbors to get real tips. Talk to tenants and landlords alike. Tenants will be much more honest about the negative aspects of a neighborhood because they haven't invested in it so there is no sentimental attachment.

Visit the neighborhood at different times of the day (and even more interesting at night), and on different days of the week to see your future neighbors.

Choice of rental property

The best real estate investment for beginners is usually a single house or a condominium. Condominiums require little maintenance because the condominium manager takes care of the repairs in the common and structural parts (such as the roof), which leaves you the worry only of the interior of the accommodation to prepare for the tenants. However, condo apartments tend to earn lower rents and appreciate more slowly than single-family homes. Single-family homes also tend to attract longer-term tenants. Families or couples are also often seen as better renters than single people because it is believed that families could be more financially stable and pay rent regularly. It's an opinion though...

Determining the rent

How is the potential rent determined? You will need to make an informed estimate. Don't get carried away by overly optimistic assumptions. Too high a rent and an empty home for months quickly reduces your overall profit and your real estate cash flow.

Start with the average neighborhood rent and work from there. Ask yourself if your home is worth a little more or a little less than average, and why. Improve the equipment and decoration of your furnished apartment to trigger a crush and obtain a higher rent. To find out if the rent amount is right for you as a real estate investor, calculate what the property will actually cost you per month in maintenance fees and taxes and deduct the minimum rent from it. From there, you will know whether your investment project is profitable enough or not.

The essential takeaways

Every region has good cities, every city has good neighborhoods, and every neighborhood has good streets. Every street has nuggets for a profitable rental investment.

It takes a lot of work and research and visits to align all the elements that determine a good rental investment with high profitability.

When you've found the perfect property, have realistic rental expectations, and make sure your prices are healthy enough that you can wait for the property to start making money without dreading any vacancy at any time of the year.

In summary...

- A low vacancy rate allows landlords to increase rents.
- Single-family homes also tend to attract longer-term tenants.

Chapter Five: Cash vs Financing

Many investors wishing to make financial investments in the real estate sector consult me frequently. Usually, they have significant capital: between $100k and $750k. But they would like to have information on the approach to adopt. They hesitate between paying cash and borrowing.

Indeed, the financing of the rental investment is done in two ways: the investor can pay cash with his own financial resources or borrow the entire amount necessary for the operation. The loan can also be a partial amount of the total sum.

The cash payment has advantages. The investor receives all of his rent as soon as his investment is made. It is exempt from reimbursements, the risk of non-reimbursement, banking fees, and formalities. It is therefore protected from the stress associated with all these operations. But he is obliged to have the entire amount needed to buy cash. And that money is locked in until the return on investment is complete. In addition, given the bulk of funds to put on the table, the investor rarely has the cash for other projects.

Despite all the uncertainties associated with borrowing, its economic interest is usually certain. In fact, rental investment with leverage makes it possible to acquire the property without committing the investor's own funds. This practice allows the latter to get rich by using the money of others. You can build up capital through debt. Your available cash remains intact and can be directed to other projects. In the event of death, your death insurance reimburses your loan, which protects your family. And your heirs receive fully purchased real estate.

In view of all these possibilities, should we opt for the cash payment or the loan? Take a quick look at the following:

1. Interest on credit

Taking out a home loan remains the best way to finance a rental investment. Logic: credit has a leverage effect. It allows you to become the owner of a property that is more difficult to pay cash for. You can thus finance housing while placing your funds in other things. Note that rental property is the only investment that can be financed with a loan. Banks won't lend you money to buy stocks...

2. A profitable investment

A second good reason to finance a rental real estate investment on credit: the interest rate of the loan is most often lower than the gross rate of return on your real estate investment. If you add capital profitability to rental yield, the overall net profitability is greater than the cost of your loan. In short: you are a beneficiary.

3. Optimized taxation

Third argument: loan interest is deductible from rents when you declare them for tax. You thus reduce your tax base, which optimizes your taxation. In addition, mortgage loans are almost always associated with death and disability insurance, which secures the operation.

Nowadays, the terms of the mortgage are good. The procedures related to credit are easy. And bank charges are low. For over 20 years, I have obtained a mortgage at a rate of 1.55%. The life insurance rate, meanwhile, is between 2.5% and 3% over the same period. It is therefore mathematically more interesting to make both a financial investment in life insurance and a mortgage for rental purposes. With regard to your investment in life insurance, you have a good argument to present to your banker as a reason to grant you the mortgage.

The preliminary steps getting financing for your property

Before embarking head-on in the search for funding, you have to think about defining your project and ask yourself the question: what do I really want? House or apartment or land that I can construct something on? These questions would allow you to define your exact need and then allow you to assess your purchasing capacity. This purchasing capacity allows you to determine how much you need to invest and borrow. It includes your borrowing capacity as well as your personal contribution that is usually needed to cover guarantee and notary fees. Once your project has been determined and the budget you want to devote to it, you can then begin your financing research.

1. You sign a contract to buy a property

You have found your property and made a purchase offer which has been accepted. The next step is to go ahead with the signing of the intent to buy the document.

This sales agreement is an official act that commits you and the seller to conclude the sale of the property in a condition and at a fixed price. The sales agreement may include a suspensive clause that determines the maximum date by which bank financing must be obtained. This period can generally be 30 to 45 days from the date of signature of the compromise. The buyer benefits from a right of withdrawal of ten days which he can exercise without needing to justify it. If you do not obtain financing before the end of the suspensive clause, the sales agreement will be canceled.

The other option is word of mouth. This differs from the signed document since it only commits the seller to reserve the property for a future buyer via trust. This is usually done in cases where the seller does not mind going with you to the bank.

2. You gather the supporting documents for your financing file

These documents relate in particular to your:

- personal situation
- credit score
- financial situation
- assets or your net worth
- current loans
- other real estate projects

They are essential for bankers because it allows them to quickly put together your file and above all to precisely analyze your situation to provide you with the most suitable solution for your project.

3. Send your financing request to various banks

You should negotiate and obtain for yourself the best rate. Together, with the bankers, find a tailor-made financing solution that allows you to take advantage of flexible and advantageous conditions concerning, for example, repayment deadlines or penalties.

4. You receive the agreement

After a study of the documents submitted, the bank will communicate to you its agreement in writing. If your request is accepted, it is essential for the continuation of your project. This agreement, in principle, is a document submitted by your bank which confirms its willingness to continue with the procedures. It is in no way the acceptance of your mortgage application. This agreement makes it possible to set in particular:

- The loan amount
- The credit rate
- The term of the loan
- Guarantees
- Conditions

In certain cases, this agreement may be accompanied by the words "subject to further review". This mention does not formally commit the bank to the offer that is proposed to you, it indicates that the bank will ask for an in-depth analysis of your file:

- Further details about your current debt level
- Statement of bank accounts
- Personal contribution

The analysis of your file and the findings that emerge from it will directly impact your mortgage application and will thus allow your lending institution to go ahead contractually or not with you. This commitment will then materialize in what is called a final agreement. Thus, the contractual loan document specifies:

- Your identity and that of the lending institution
- The characteristics of the mortgage loan: Amount, duration, personal contribution
- The repayment terms
- Guarantee and insurance costs
- General and specific conditions

5. You sign the loan offer

The contractual loan document issued by the lending bank seals the precise provisions of your financing. The loan offer is valid for a period of 30 days during which the bank cannot modify the conditions of the offer. To be valid, the offer must be accepted after a minimum period of reflection of 10 calendar days. Before the expiry date of the offer and after the reflection period, you will therefore have to return the signed loan offer to the bank to signify your agreement.

Be aware that when you take out a mortgage with a bank, the latter may ask you to open a bank account to domiciliate your income with them in part or in full.

6. You sign the deed of sale with a notary

The signing of the deed of sale is the last step to formalize the real estate transaction. Carried out by a notary, this document confirms the information present in the contract such as contact details, characteristics of the property, mandatory diagnoses, price, notary fees, or guarantees. Beforehand, these various data are verified by the notary. After the funds have been transferred, the deed of sale will be registered by a notary and you will receive your title deed and keys. You, therefore, become the owner of the property that you have been coveting for a few months.

For construction work, the funds will be released as and when the work progresses.

7. You own and repay your loan

You take advantage of the property acquired and start repaying your first monthly payment either one month after signing or deferred according to the conditions set by your mortgage.

In summary...

- Interest on credit Taking out a home loan remains the best way to finance a rental investment.
- A mortgage loan is almost always associated with death and disability insurance, which secures the operation. It is therefore mathematically more interesting to make both a financial investment in life insurance

and a mortgage for rental purposes.
- Together, with the bankers, find a tailor-made financing solution that allows you to take advantage of flexible and advantageous conditions concerning, for example, repayment deadlines or penalties.

Chapter Six: Real Estate Financing Options

Obtaining credit without having to go through the services of a bank is possible. Indeed, for several years, the services which propose to bypass the traditional banking intermediation multiply. Here is an overview of the different solutions available to you if you want to carry out a project using others' credit without going through a bank.

To carry out a project, whether it is the purchase of a car, the financing of a trip or even work in your home, you may need a loan. Indeed, if you do not have the necessary savings aside, borrowing and repaying over time is an excellent solution.

Soliciting financial institutions (banks or specialized credit organizations) is often the first reflex for consumers. Logical, because the banks concentrate most of the loans granted today. But other alternative solutions are emerging to help households.

Loans between individuals have multiplied, but also crowdfunding allows certain projects to be carried out. In addition, there is also microcredit, which allows people excluded from the traditional banking system loans in several countries to be able to borrow.

Borrowing without a bank is therefore possible, both out of obligation for people who cannot obtain loans from traditional banks or by choice, for people who wish to follow up with an intermediary.

Is getting a bank credit practical?

Securing financing for real estate properties on the scale required is one of the most important for any real estate development project and therefore for every developer. One of the important features of real estate is its high capital intensity. Since real estate is an expensive commodity, its purchase or construction requires a significant amount of capital investment. Raising funds for the purchase or construction of a real estate object is, on the one hand, an important measure, and on the other, an element of the formation of the profitability of returns on such an investment.

The results of the theoretical study regarding the sources, methods, and forms of financing real estate objects showed the following:

- Both the number of financing methods and their composition vary.
- There are certain lexical differences in the names of financing methods.
- Often the forms of financing differ little from the methods.

Thus, we consider it expedient to single out the methods of financing, and in them - the forms of financing, which consist of sources of financing.

Funding Methods	*Funding Method Features*
Self-financing	Financing exclusively from own funds
Shareholding	Financing through transactions with stocks and other securities
Loan financing	Financing on the terms of repayment
Consortium financing	Financing by combining opportunitie with other business entities
Leasing and selling	Financing not in cash, but with owne material on certain conditions
Concessional financing	Financing on terms that are significantly more profitable than those existing on the market
Subsidizing	Financing on a no-return basis
Blended finance	Financing through a combination of several financing methods

Lending money directly between individuals is also possible. This is not, moreover, a novelty. With family or friends, it is possible to lend each other money.

For the US market, there are eight potential real estate financing solutions available that do not involve banks.

Portfolio Loans are the first type of loan.

In contrast to conventional mortgages, portfolio loans are not resold on the secondary market to large financial institutions such as Fannie Mae and Freddie Mac. So instead of being compelled to obey the rigorous guidelines imposed by the secondary buyer, lenders are given the freedom to set whatever terms they deem appropriate. Portfolio loans, as opposed to typical mortgages, may be easier to obtain for investors and self-employed borrowers as a result of this. Because most lenders who deal in portfolio loans do not publicize their services, it is essential to seek a lender through recommendations, investor networks, and other means. Otherwise, you will simply have to contact each lender and inquire directly as to whether or not they offer portfolio loans.

Federal Housing Administration Loans are the second type of loan.

When it comes to mortgages held by banks all around the country, the Federal Housing Administration is involved, and they also offer a program to assist people in purchasing homes in which they expect to live permanently. As a result, an FHA-backed loan does not apply to "investment property" in the strictest sense. The exception clause, on the other hand, permits you to utilize an FHA loan to purchase a home with up to four units if you live in only one of them, according to the FHA. The fact that this sort of loan requires a minimal down payment of only 3.5 percent is the primary attraction.

203K Loans are the third type of loan.

In most areas, a 203K loan is identical to an FHA loan in terms of its terms and conditions. It varies from the others, though, in that it allows you to borrow additional funds to use in rehabilitation and restoration tasks. This additional cash is included in the original real estate financing, which makes it extremely easy.

Owner Financing is the fourth option.

It is possible to avoid costly bank fees and make payments directly to the homeowner if you can locate a homeowner who owns his home outright, wants to sell, and is prepared to offer the financing. You will almost certainly have to pay a higher interest rate, but the transaction will be completed more quickly and easily.

Hard Money Loans are a type of loan that is difficult to obtain. It is however possible so it is our fifth option.

A "hard money" loan is made by a private business or investor, rather than a bank, for the aim of making a short-term financial investment. These loans, however, carry a high level of risk, providing investors with the opportunity to make a quick profit by flipping or refurbishing profitable homes. Furthermore, because hard money loans are typically handled quickly, they make it easier to acquire such assets before it is too late. It will be determined whether or not to provide the loan primarily based on the property's market worth, rather than based on collateral. The interest rate is greater than average, ranging from 8 percent to 15 percent, with a time span ranging from 6 months to 3 years.

Personal Loans with Confidentiality is the sixth option.

These loans are similar to hard money loans, except that the lender and borrower have a more personal relationship with one another. Because of this relationship, it is easier to reach an agreement on conditions that are acceptable to both parties, and the interest rate, points, and fees are often significantly cheaper. If the borrower fails to meet his or her commitments, the lender may still foreclose on the property.

Home equity financing is the seventh option.

Taking a home equity loan is often more convenient than applying for a new loan if you already own a piece of real estate and have built up significant equity in it. This can be in the form of a loan (HEIL) or a line of credit (HELOC), and banks are typically willing to accept you if you have a significant amount of equity built up in your property. The bank will only lend a set proportion of the overall value of your existing property, minus the amount you still owe on that property, usually 90 percent of that value. This is frequently sufficient to cover at least a portion of the down payment on the new property you are considering. You may be able to deduct the interest you paid on the loan from your taxes as well.

Commercial Loans are number eight on the list.

Other than residential real estate financing, the other seven strategies stated above can also be employed for commercial real estate finance, which can be very lucrative. A commercial loan will typically have a higher rate of interest and fees, as well as a shorter repayment period. For commercial real estate flipping, a business line of credit is another option to consider. While the income level of the borrower is typically the most important approval requirement for other types of loans, the revenue that the property is deemed capable of generating is the most important consideration for commercial loans. Your financial abilities as well as your previous experience in the field of commercial real estate investment will be extensively reviewed as well.

Crowdfunding to avoid banks is the ninth option.

Another solution to avoid banks, crowdfunding. If you want to carry out a personal project that may interest other people, then you can ask for help, including financial participation! When the repayment occurs in the context of crowdfunding, we call it crowdlending.

With crowdfunding, it is even possible for some individuals to make a capital or equity investment, that is to say, to take shares in the project or the company financed with the help of crowdfunding.

The collection of financial donations as a loan is the tenth option.

While originally, most crowdfunding platforms allowed members to propose projects with a social or solitary dimension, today it is easy to offer all initiatives. A personal project, a real estate project, the creation of a start-up, or the financing of a trip…almost anything goes.

Many projects are thus financed thanks to donations, without any compensation. It is sometimes possible to give a reward, with a gift, a promotional item, or even a thank you symbolically.

In summary...

- Obtaining credit without having to go through the services of a bank is possible.

Chapter Seven: Real Estate Investment Strategies

R. Kiyosaki said: "I do not want to sell my property, I want it to bring me money every month, over and over again." Our task will be to find as much as possible such properties that will give us not a one-time profit, but a constant, monthly, annual, hundred-year, thousand-year income, without our participation. This is our goal!

Real estate is constantly growing in value. In 2022, 2030, and 2050 real estate will grow in value and generate income! You can see the statistics on the growth of real estate prices worldwide. People are still buying apartments, houses, land plots, and many make huge fortunes on this. Will you be among them? It's up to you to decide!

Many of the strategies discussed in this chapter work in both boom and bust. But our task is not just to buy and sell, our task is to buy and receive money from a property for life. Buy-sell speculation is not the best system, as it is often associated with market dependence. It can also prove to be much riskier than the ones we'll talk about below.

Important note! These strategies can be mixed, superimposed on one another, added as a part of one to another, deal with several at once, in stages, it all depends on how you see this business. There is always a strategy to increase profits and reduce costs. The main thing in all this is to understand that there is no ideal strategy, the main thing is to do it. Better to do fairly, but do, than do nothing well! Remember this.

Enough words, let's get down to business!

Strategy No. 1. Purchase - Renovation - Sale

This strategy is just one of those that allow you to make money as quickly as possible, capitalize your income, and enter another, more profitable project. This strategy can be used as a set of the money supply.

How to sell without money? Example: You find a friend, partner, investor, offer him to buy an apartment. It can be an old apartment, "killed", or a new building that needs renovation. Doing repairs with your own hands or by hiring workers. In a month you hand over the property and get 50% of the difference (profit) in money.

Several such apartments and you will already buy an apartment with your own money. These may be new buildings, secondary housing, or old houses. The main thing is to understand the scheme itself. We take without repair - cheap, we sell with repair - expensive! Here you can also make a lot of studios out of it or rent it daily and share the profit with the investor (the one who gave you the money). The main thing is not to forget to draw up all the agreements with a notary so that later there will be no scandals when you are asked to leave. Always reassure everything.

The downside here is that you can mess with the budget and not meet it. The main thing in all strategies, whatever you do, is the miscalculation, monitoring, and testing of the market. I will also touch on this topic further.

Strategy No. 2. New buildings

At the stage of the foundation, there are simply cosmic discounts, installments, mortgages. Having bought an apartment at the construction stage, the apartment will cost you much less than the same in the completed version. The selling technology can also be applied here, even during the construction phase. In just 1 year, a property can grow in price several times. Many are engaged in buying and selling in this niche.

What strategies should you use? You can also buy at a less complete stage then, you can wait for the completion of the construction and rent it, dividing it into studios. You can rent it daily, make a hostel, if this is the ground floor, then you can transfer the property to a non-residential fund and rent the apartment as a store.

There are two drawbacks here. The first is that you have to wait at least a year for the building to be built and put into operation. Second, the fact that while you wait for the construction, the property can be frozen and then it becomes a headache, and not a business. Carefully choose a trusted and reliable builder who doesn't have problems.

Strategy No. 3. Alteration of an apartment to a mini studio

The goal of this strategy, regardless of whether you have an apartment, a house, or a townhouse, is the maximum division into studios and subsequent rent. This strategy is one of the profitable ones. We have a piece, we divide this piece into small pieces and hand them over. If we add money from small pieces, it turns out much more than if we hand over a whole piece.

For example, a one-room apartment can bring, say, 3,000 dollars per month, if we divide it into studios, then we get at least 2, often even 3 studios. So we can rent a smaller studio for 1,800, and another large studio for 2,000 dollars. In general, we get 3,800 dollars. If we manage to make another third, then this is another 1,500 dollars. Total: we get 5,300 dollars from an apartment divided into a studio, instead of 3,000 dollars from the whole apartment! This is 2,300 dollars per month more than they rent on the market. This is +27,600 dollars per year of extra money. And if you have several such apartments?

With this strategy, the mortgage goes well. Example: So if we buy an apartment on a mortgage and pay 3,500 dollars from it every month, and we get 5,300 dollars from renting out the studios, then this mortgage is paid not by you, but by the tenants, plus you earn 1,800 dollars on top. And if you have several such apartments or houses?

Strategy No. 4. Unfinished

If you correctly calculate and bend the owner well for a discount, pointing out the dented jambs, etc, then you can make a decent cash flow. Different strategies can be applied here. You can make studios and rent them out, you can make a hotel, rent it out for rent, or make a hostel.

You can use crowd-investing (public investment) or pooling (equity participation) and finish building a house with someone else's money and hands. You can live on one of the floors, and rent the rest. This is just a part of what you can do, use your imagination and calculate everything.

The disadvantage that may arise is to miscalculate the repair and completion. This is not a cheap business, so calculate everything at once so that you know where each dollar you have to spare will go.

When we arrived in the town of Denver, Colorado Region, there was a 2-story unfinished building near our house. It stood there for about eight years. I don't know how long it stood before that, but the point is that in 2014 it was bought out and completed. Now it is a tire service and a car shop.

Judging by what kind of movement there is all the time and the fact that someone is using the place and, being a business, renovates it all the time, we can conclude that the buyer made the right decision with the choice of buying the dilapidated place. It's nice to see that this building is now operational and not a bottle and rubbish warehouse.

Strategy No. 5. Transfer from residential to non-residential

The strategy is especially beneficial for those who are engaged in their own business and develop it, looking for a cheap rental space or, in general, for this space to be their own. There is also a whole industry here.

You can use the strategy to rent out premises to other businessmen. In such premises, you can often see shops, here you can also attach all sorts of additional premises, making the property larger.

Here, you can buy a huge room, with high ceilings, with the possibility of completing the second floor, increasing the area, and hence the profit at least twice. The main thing here is to find a place suitable for settling people. You can make hostels, premises for cafes, dormitories for students out of such properties. You can mix strategies. Again, it all depends on what is available to you - what you see. It is then up to you to squeeze money out of every meter as much as possible. Basements are sometimes used for hostels. If you include attention and imagination, then you can also see that money is literally under your feet.

The disadvantage of this strategy is that it can take time and additional money, but if you have a team, then this is all solved and rather quickly.

Strategy No. 6. Large offices to mini-offices

Like Strategy No. 3, dividing the office gives us more profit than if we rented it in its entirety. In general, any strategy with dividing a big one into a small one and then selling or renting small parts of it gives more profit. Whether it's buying cars and selling them for parts, or dividing a company into shares, or buying in bulk, selling at retail, this strategy is as old as the world. Buy a large one, split it into many small pieces, and you will have more profit.

Here you can also apply the strategy of subletting the premises with the consent of the owner to demarcate his premises. Then it will cost you even less, and the net profit will be made faster, without using extra (your) money.

The disadvantage of this strategy is only that you need to find a good place where there is a demand for offices, as well as take into account the scale of the rework, but if there is a team, then you can always find those who will do it for you.

Strategy No. 7. Office by the hour

Now that we have divided the offices, you can rent some of them for an hour or more. As with dividing space, dividing the time of change also makes more money than just rent for a month. This applies to both apartments, houses, and commercial real estate. Everything that can be divided - we divide, everything that can be handed over and take more for it - we embody!

In order to understand how this works, we will use an example. Here we have an office, it can bring 4,000 dollars a month, we rent it by the hour (for negotiations, business meetings, etc.), for example, an hour will cost 50 dollars, which is very little. But let's calculate that the offices work 22 days, 10 hours each, out of these 10 hours we take 80% (with sufficient advertising) and multiply by 22 days. 22 x 8 = 176. Now we multiply 176 (this is a month) hours by 50 dollars per hour, 176 x 50 = 8,800 dollars! Not bad math, don't you agree? The difference in delivery monthly and hourly is 4,800 dollars! This is 57,600 dollars per year from only one office rented by the hour. And if you have several of them?

The disadvantage of this strategy is in setting up advertising as you need a constant flow of customers. You also need a team to help you with the organizational work with customers.

Strategy No. 8. Daily sublease of apartments

A huge plus of this strategy is that you can start without your own apartments and with minimal investment. I know people who started this real estate business with this strategy without investing anything at all, and it works.

The strategy is simple, we rent an apartment on a monthly basis (for a long period) with the right to sublease (the right to re-rent it to others) and rent it out by the day. Having hired the necessary staff, you do not need to be present in this business at all, even apartments will be looked for and launched without your participation. It all depends on the setup of the process. The profitability of this business can be up to 200% per month! You can always find tenants looking for short-term stay via websites like AirBnB, Expedia, and hotels.com, etc.

There is only one minus here, in finding clients and adjusting for the permanent occupancy of apartments. Having set this up, you will not have to worry about the settlements anymore and will only have to increase the number of apartments, getting more and more money.

Strategy No. 9. Dorms and hostels

Here are the hostels, really worth considering as a business model of the future. Hostels rule! This is not just a place where you can throw the dice like school kids, it is a whole community, a get-together of travelers, creative people, those who are interested in finding new acquaintances and spending time with interesting activities. The hostels have the Internet, all communications, all equipment, a place for board games, and most importantly, each hostel has its own extra attractions around its location that attract people like a magnet. Now the topic of capsule hotels has begun to develop, these are also hostels, but at a different level.

Remember, I said that dividing the space and time into separate pieces gives more profit, and so, hostels are the most profitable of these divisions, here you can place a three-tiered bed on two square meters and earn more from 1 square meter than from daily rent or delivery of mini offices by the hour.

The disadvantage of this strategy is in finding suitable premises and its equipment. Good investments are also required, but if there is a strategy, a team, and an investor, then you can always do everything with someone else's hands and money, getting a piece of the business. The main thing is to correctly calculate everything, test and organize the process, bringing it to the result! There are millions of dollars in this strategy!

Strategy No. 10. Townhouses, duplexes, quad houses

It is important to calculate everything here, in principle, as elsewhere. The main idea of buying a townhouse is that it is a turnkey house and the price segment is quite high, which means that clients who will rent a house are ready to pay. Here, the strategy of dividing into studios and renting for a long time, daily rent, can be additionally attached to the house, thereby increasing your profit. You can rent a part and live in the same house. You can come up with different options with additional functions, for example, the Internet, parking for which people are willing to pay. The mortgage strategy also applies here. The rent for housing will be enough for you to cover the mortgage and so that you have a couple of hundred dollars left every month.

The disadvantage of the strategy is that it requires a fairly large entry for the money. If you use a mortgage, then everything will come out much cheaper. The main thing is to calculate everything so that you do not run and frantically look for money. Connect your partners, investors, and, of course, your head!

Strategy No. 11. Country estate

Many people build companies on this strategy. Suburban real estate is in demand and will grow as cities grow. A moment comes when the city begins to grow tiresome and a person is looking for where to rest, to be closer to nature, but without giving up the benefits of civilization. This is where business begins for you.

The system is simple, buy inexpensively, divide into studios, attach or sublet and rent. Around nature, farther from noise. Ecotourism. There is a demand for this, and it continues to grow. In general, ecotourism is a new direction for many people and you will make money on it. Houses can be purchased not only outside the city but also near beaches and resort areas.

This business is for those who want to be away from the city and at the same time do business. For such people, this strategy is ideal. Again, here you can mix different ways of renting, subletting, dividing, outbuildings, and other things, you need to calculate everything and look at the terrain.

The disadvantage of this system is, of course, in the clients. The price of houses outside the city is small, but the main thing is to learn how to attract a good customer flow. If calculated correctly, this will give an excellent profit and a lot of pleasant emotions, and if this house is owned somewhere on the seashore, then it is simply gorgeous. I would have lived there. Yes. Take unfinished buildings in resort areas, rent, and live there. Take action!

Strategy No. 12. We build a cheap house, quickly and share

This is one of those strategies that our family and team regularly implement. I really like it, and now I will tell you why.

I love to create, I love to make candy out of garbage and sell it for more than what it was before. Or, to put it another way, do you know about the world-famous Peugeot ad in India? If you don't, I'll tell you.

A young Indian drives up to an elephant in his car. The car is very old. And so he sits in the cabin of his car and looks at a picture of a new Peugeot (Peugeot 206) and then starts. He crashes the car into the wall in front, then reverses, then he puts the elephant on the car in the right places, and voila, he has a new Peugeot 206, or almost new...

If you don't know what I am talking about, then type in the YouTube search bar: Peugeot 206 commercial - India. The advertising is very revealing.

So, the construction of cheap houses is very similar to this advertisement, with the only difference being that we will have fairly high-quality houses, and we will rent them above market value due to the location and beauty of the interior, exterior, and services provided.

This strategy is mixed with many, here you can buy land anywhere (the main thing is to calculate the profit), you can build from used port containers, foam plastic, adobe (a mixture of clay and straw), etc. By the way, the latter method is very environmentally friendly, so I would recommend everyone to live in houses and raise their children in them.

After construction, we launch the house and rent it out, daily, monthly, or as a hostel. If you choose the right place (near the city), then you will always have 100% occupancy, and the profit is simply cosmic.

This business is easily scalable and very creative. Here your task will be in choosing the land, what the house will be like, how to make more profit by building a large house that covers most of the land plot. It's a great strategy and I like it.

There is only one minus here, in that construction requires money, but again, by attracting investors and the right people who are ready to enter into a share, you can very quickly put together capital for yourself.

The construction and commissioning of such a house can take about a month, which is very cool, since the sooner we launch a business, the faster it pays off and begins to bring us a profit.

Strategy number 13. Overseas property

With this strategy, you don't have to be afraid of economic crises in your home country. You can travel and live in your own properties. This is a great strategy for diversifying your portfolio, where you will have not only real estate in your homeland, but also, say, Thailand, India, China, UAE, UK, Spain, Greece, Bulgaria, Cyprus, Turkey, or even Brazil.

Such real estate can yield profit both from 100% per year and from 100% per month, depending on the location and your strategy. The countries that I indicated above are now popular for investment, if you can't sit still, then take this strategy and go ahead, conquer the countries! Here, as well as with other systems, you can do business both on construction, and on delivery, and on sublease, as well as in other ways. By switching on your brain, you will find money, people, and all the resources.

The disadvantage of this strategy is that in the country in which you have an investment property, there may be a war, crisis, or other, then it will not have a very good effect on your business. But from any situation, you can always find a way out and benefit, therefore, calculate everything and develop your investment strategy.

Strategy No. 14. Auction properties

This is a cool strategy where you can buy land, houses, apartments for very low prices. By the way, not only houses but also equipment, cars and a whole bunch of other things, even loans. Knowing how it works, you can use all the strategies along with this one. If you know where and what to look for, and what it can bring, then this will give you a huge advantage over other businessmen and investors.

In summary...

- You can make studios and rent them out, you can make a hostel, etc., In 2022, 2030, and 2050, real estate will grow in value and generate income!

Chapter Eight: How To Prepare a Successful Real Estate Business Plan

All businesses (firms, companies) need a business plan. This chapter is about real estate business plans, about the problems associated with its development. It is a useful help for readers who are just going to create a new real estate enterprise, as well as those who are no longer new to the business but want to expand its scope, modify or supplement the directions of their activities.

A real estate business plan is a planning document. It is important, after all, planning is a process of creative understanding of the future of your enterprise (business). At this time, you decide: in which direction to develop your business and how quickly, how to achieve your goals and what to do to reduce possible surprises and risks, how to manage the situation as a whole. In other words, effective planning is the process of setting goals (objectives) and developing activities to ensure their achievement.

A real estate business plan is necessarily a written document that summarizes business opportunities and prospects and explains how these opportunities can be implemented by the existing team of managers and staff. Writing a real estate business plan makes the process of developing it more efficient, and the plan itself - systematized and concise.

Mastering the art of developing a real estate business plan is necessary for at least the following five reasons:

1. The new economic conditions require new entrepreneurs and allow them to try to realize their "entrepreneurial inclinations". However, many of these people have never run any commercial enterprise and therefore have very little understanding of the whole range of problems associated with entrepreneurship in a market economy;

2. The changing economic environment also confronts experienced heads of enterprises with the need to calculate their future steps in a different way and prepare for an unusual struggle with competitors, in which there should be no room for lackluster attitudes.

3. The real estate business plan is the link between you and the investor. If an entrepreneur counts not only on his own funds but wants to attract funds from outside, that is, to interest potential investors, including foreign ones, to invest in the proposed business, it is necessary to show them the effectiveness of such an investment. Your ability to think realistically and evaluate all possible aspects, both positive and negative, of the use of the invested funds.

    If you apply for the necessary funds at a bank, you will also need a real estate business plan that will help convince the banker of the reliability of the investment, the reality of the return of the loan issued to you, and the receipt of your profit. In this case, the real estate business plan is a "for sale" document to receive capital. In the "selling" real estate business plan, you need to slightly change the emphasis, for example, be sure to include the basic biographical information of the prospective managers, information about their education and work experience. This information is key to potential investors. Actually, the purpose of a real estate business plan is usually the main one for anyone that needs to raise capital. The real estate business plan must convince investors that the new entrepreneur has realistically identified his opportunities, has the entrepreneurial and managerial talent to seize these opportunities, and has a reasonably realistic, consistent program for generating profits and achieving goals over time.

    And if you do not need borrowed funds? If you have enough capital to start your own business without attracting outside investors? Do you need a real estate business plan in this case? In this case, too, a real estate business plan is necessary. It is necessary to separate two processes: planning and investing. An entrepreneur who has the means must write a real estate business plan not "for sale", but for himself. In this case, you will receive the benefits described below (fourth, and fifth)

4. The real estate business plan will allow, first of all, you to clearly see the prospects of your business, assess the existing economic situation and your opportunities, determine effective directions for the development of the company, and all the necessary actions to achieve

the set goals, analyze your ideas, check them with reasonableness and realism. In this regard, not only the final result of this planned work - a complete real estate business plan but also the process of developing a real estate business plan itself is valuable. All involved in it receive an excellent experience of future joint activities and communication, as well as a well-grounded motivated view of the prospects for business development.

5. The real estate business plan will serve as a standard for you and your employees against which you will check the results of practical activities for its implementation and make the necessary adjustments to this activity. It will allow employees to clearly understand their tasks and see their own personal prospects associated with a common business for all, and assess their contribution to achieving the set goals. The real estate business plan will prove to be useful for setting priorities and individual work assignments for the first year of the enterprise.

Consider the developed real estate business plan as a "flight map" that defines the most desirable, optimal in time, and least risky route to achieve the intended goals.

However, numerous factors, including such as "unexpected weather change" can significantly change the plans. For first-timers, it is common practice to deviate from the route outlined in the real estate business plan. Try to anticipate possible deviations, develop "fallbacks" and prepare "side routes". After all, in the end, it has long been known that a plan that does not tolerate modifications is bad.

Who develops the real estate business plan?

The answer to this question can be very short - the main character (or persons). The planning must be carried out by the current or future leaders of the company. Then there are those who will take responsibility for the implementation of the real estate business plan. Let's try to expand our answer and explain its categorical nature.

The personal participation of the head (current or potential) in the preparation of the real estate business plan is so important that many investors refuse to consider applications for the allocation of funds at all if it becomes known that the real estate business plan was prepared from the beginning to the end by an outside consultant, and the head only signed ...

This does not mean, of course, that it is not necessary to use the services of consultants - quite the contrary, the involvement of experts is highly welcomed by investors. However, by being involved in this work personally, you kind of simulate your future activities, checking the strength of the plan itself and yourself - will you have enough strength to bring the matter to a successful conclusion and move on? On the other hand, you show the investor the level of your qualifications, you are also showing your willingness to be entrepreneurial.

If you are in doubt about your literary talents, ask someone to edit the finished real estate business plan to correct grammatical errors, but do not avoid the process of creating the real estate business plan itself. The time spent on its preparation is not wasted: this is the time that you have already devoted to your future business. You are already working for your future. Developing real estate business plans is exactly what you should do. Every time you develop a real estate business plan, you become an increasingly experienced entrepreneur.

In the process of preparing a real estate business plan, based on the analysis and calculations performed, you can radically change your initial decision.

Many entrepreneurs, not being able to state the main thing, write too much (up to 200 pages). Full of unnecessary details. As a result, such real estate business plans are less effective than they could be.

Firstly, the excessive volume of the real estate business plan makes it difficult to understand the essence of the ideas presented in it, and secondly, this real estate business plan is unlikely to be read carefully.

Consider the problem of familiarizing yourself with a 200-page real estate business plan from the perspective of an investor (after all, an investor is exactly the person to whom you want to "sell" your real estate business plan). For several investment firms, even a medium-sized enterprise receives several dozen real estate business plans every week. How does the prospective investor behave in this case? Four out of five real estate business plans will be passed or paused no more than 10-15 minutes after a quick scan. Of the rest, again four out of five will be read a little more attentively and longer (an hour or more) and again put aside. And only the rest of the total number of submitted real estate business plans (approximately one out of a hundred) will be signed and in the future will become the subject of serious negotiations, as a result of which, at best, one of the signed real estate business plans will be invested in.

As for advice, the optimal volume of a real estate business plan is no more than 35-40 pages. Do not overload it with diagrams and pictures for the purpose of "learning". Use only those illustrations or diagrams, without which it is difficult to understand the content of the real estate business plan. The appearance of the plan should not be an end in itself, the main thing is the accessibility of understanding its content.

And, of course, the real estate business plan should have a title page and a table of contents. The title page contains the name of the company (or the name and surname of the potential entrepreneur, if there is no company yet), address, email address, and telephone (or fax) number. It is desirable to place the table of contents on one page. This is a very important part of a real estate business plan. Each of the readers has his own, the most interesting moments that he wants to immediately find out, for example, the number of required investments, the timing of their return. The table of contents will immediately tell the reader where to find this information. The pages of the real estate business plan must be numbered and put down next to the names of the sections in the table of contents.

Components of your real estate business plan

Real estate business plans start from the end – with a summary. This is a crucial part of your real estate business plan. For many real estate business plans this is the only section that will be read by a potential investor, after which the real estate business plan will be put aside. This means that the "brief conclusions" could turn out to be unconvincing and not interest the investor. Summaries allow the reader to understand the basic ideas and prospects of your business quickly and decide whether to spend the extra time reading your plan. Consequently, the purpose of short conclusions (summaries) is to interest and even "seduce" the potential reader.

To do this, you must be able to convey your optimism towards your business to the reader. To do this, you do not need to use "slogans", just demonstrate in a benevolent, confidential tone that you are ready and able to use all the opportunities provided by the market to achieve success.

Summary conclusions are the essence of your proposal, this is the result of an already written real estate business plan. Here, on one or two (maximum three) pages, the essence of your business should be presented in an extremely simple and concise manner: what are you going to do, how your future product (service) will differ from competitors' products and why consumers will be interested in it, what costs (investments) will be required for the implementation of your project and sources of their receipt. Here you must provide digital data on the volume of future sales (in the next 3-5 years), revenue, profit, the level of profitability, and, finally, the period during which you can be guaranteed to return all borrowed funds (or in other words, the payback period of the capital investment).

As follows from the contents of the "Brief Conclusions", they, of course, are written after the real estate business plan is fully prepared, all its sections are calculated, and you, together with your employees and involved consultants, have achieved complete clarity in all the details of your project. Depending on the nature of your business and the capabilities of the writer, you can prepare two types of summary conclusions: concise or descriptive.

Concise summary conclusions are more straightforward and "frank" for two reasons: they simply repeat in abbreviated form the conclusions of each section of the real estate business plan. The advantage of such short conclusions is that they are easy to write and are least dependent on the ability of the writer. The only drawback of concise summary conclusions is a too "dry", business tone. The executive summary covers all sections of your real estate business plan and presents them equally, albeit abbreviated.

Brief descriptive conclusions are like a short story that you present to the reader. Here you can describe your business with great drama and excitement. However, it is necessary to have 'sufficient ability to present the required information, arouse the enthusiasm of the reader and not fall into exaggeration. With these succinct summaries, you can evoke an emotional response from the reader by citing one or two of the most impressive traits of your company and showing how these traits will contribute to the success of your future business.

The order of presentation of the material in the brief summary is arbitrary. In this case, for example, the concept of your business can be described in three paragraphs, and the management team - in one or two sentences. It all depends on what you pay more attention to. They should, however, give your investors all the information they need.

In summary...

- Consider the developed real estate business plan as a "flight map" that defines the most desirable, optimal in time, and least risky route to achieve the intended goals. However, it is necessary to have sufficient ability whilst presenting the required information, arousing the enthusiasm of the reader and not falling into exaggeration.

Chapter Nine: I Understand the Market: A Simple Guide to Convincing Investors

In this chapter, which opens the main part of the real estate business plan, a detailed description of the future, product, or service that you want to offer to buyers (consumers) is given. Here you set out your "main idea". When developing this section, it is required to answer very clearly a number of questions:

- What needs is your product (or service) intended to satisfy?
- What is special about it and why will consumers distinguish it from the products and services provided by other companies and give preference to it?
- Why did you choose this product (service) and this market, how are they attractive to you?
- What is the product life cycle or, in other words, how soon will it become obsolete?

The correct answers to the first two questions require a clear understanding of what buyers actually acquire when renting a particular place. This is the core of the concept of a product and without visualizing it, it is impossible to correctly develop the "product" itself.

Let's think about it. What do we get when we buy toothpaste? What is our need? Do we just want to buy this tube? Of course not. When we buy toothpaste, we buy healthy teeth, a feeling of freshness, and a charming smile. This is precisely our need for toothpaste. Head of the renowned cosmetics firm Revlon, Inc. believes: "In the factory we make cosmetics. In the store we sell hope."

For the third question, be sure to state your core abilities and skills and how they influenced your business choices.

For the success of a real estate business plan, it is advisable to include a photograph or a very good drawing of the housing type in it, allowing you to make and portray a clear idea about it.

If your real estate business plan is about a hostel or a high-end property, do not forget to describe the "after-sales" service system. In general, in this section of the real estate business plan, try to describe the range of additional services provided to the renter. That is the "reinforcement" that makes you different from the competition.

And the finishing touch of this section of the real estate business plan is a set of data on the estimated price of the units, the cost of its purchase, maintenance, and the amount of profit brought by each unit in the building.

Goals and strategy

Briefly outline the goals you will strive for in your business for the next three years and the overall strategy for achieving them. Three years is, of course, not the end of the road. However, according to many experts, a realistic forecast for more than three years is practically impossible due to the rapidly changing market situation.

Even three years is a long enough period. You need to focus on the most important goals and not get too detailed. The means to achieve this is to establish (define) one goal for each component of your business: market, money, production, people, location, etc. These goals should clearly define the desired outcome (for example, an increase in rent by 20% annually). When all the goals are formulated, describe the ways to achieve them.

Once again, I remind you: limit yourself to one main goal for each part of the business. By citing more goals, you risk getting bogged down in details and confusing the presentation or you may give the impression of a person who is going to achieve too much, which is not realistic. Real estate business plan development is impossible without priorities. And don't be in a hurry! For a start-up company, too high a development rate is dangerous.

Market description

The key to business success is knowing your customers or, in other words, your market. After all, if you don't know who your customers are, how can you understand their needs? Success depends on your ability to anticipate the needs and demands of consumers, which means that you must know who your consumers are, what they want, where they would like to live, and what they can afford. In addition, if you want to maximize the security of your investment, disregard for the nature and size of the market is unforgivable. Many investors prefer individuals/companies already known well oriented with the market, compared to people with limited knowledge of their proposed future real estate investment locations. Therefore, your knowledge of the market should be reflected as well as possible in the real estate business plan.

A good market analysis can lead to changes in locations, apartment structure, and even affect the nature of rental duration. Ultimately, a good market analysis will save you money. Deciding which of the marketing mechanisms to activate (advertising online, for rent billboards, etc.), you should choose the direction that most closely matches your target market.

Experience shows that the failure of most failed commercial events was because entrepreneurs did not have a clear answer to the questions: What market do they want to offer their product to? Who will buy this product, why, and for how much?

This section of the real estate business plan should provide answers to these difficult questions, based on the performed studies of the existing market, forecasting it, at least for the next 2-3 years, as well as studying the role of possible competition that you will have to face when renting your units.

If you do not rent your product directly to the tenants, but use channels such as realtors and house agents, you must develop two marketing plans because you have two markets: the end consumer market and the intermediary market. These two markets may have their own characteristics that must be understood and taken into account by you.

You can use the services of specialists in the field of marketing research, advertising, and public relations. And while these specialists can greatly increase the effectiveness of your efforts, in any case, do not entrust them completely with the development of a marketing program. It is too risky for your business to succeed.

How to get information about "your" market

Sources of such information may be existing and available data on the rental rates of similar units by competitors, the quality and sizes of their units, as well as extra amenities and services provided. You will also need such information when preparing the next section of the "Competitors" real estate business plan to better convince your investors.

Where can I get such data? The information you need can be obtained via word of mouth in the neighborhood that you decide to invest in. As noted earlier, you could also use the services of specialists in the field of marketing research, advertising, and public relations.

Marketing research objectives can be exploratory, descriptive, experimental. Search goals involve the collection of preliminary data that clarify current problems, and often help to develop or refine a hypothesis. Descriptive goals provide for the description of a certain phenomenon, for example, the number of renters of a certain unit type, the characteristics of the beliefs and preferences of people, the purchasing strength of the renters. Experimental goals involve testing the hypothesis that we have developed, for example, that a 5% decrease in prices for a given apartment type will lead to an increase in renter preference for the same by 10%.

Having worked out the purpose of the study, it is necessary to determine the sources of the information required for its implementation. According to the method of obtaining data, information is divided into primary - collected for the first time for this study, and secondary - already available information, collected centrally or for other purposes. Secondary information is usually the starting point of research, it is publicly available (for example, published statistics).

Obtaining the information you need may require careful market segmentation. As each street is different, even when supposedly close to each other, this segmentation will help you formulate your marketing research plan correctly and prepare a well-grounded description of the market for your "product".

Questions to ask yourself

I clearly understand that performing such a large amount of work on market analysis and obtaining the information necessary is a lot of work. However, it is important. To be sure that you are being practical and realistic with your analysis, try to ask yourself the following questions and give the most objective answers to them:

- Do you know which markets are the most profitable?
- Do you have an idea of how the competition will develop and how do you assess your advantages and weaknesses in the face of competition?
- Do you understand clearly enough the possibility of the emergence of new competitors, new units - substitutes on the market, or new groups of consumers?
- Will you be able to easily adapt to the expected changes, the emergence of new products - units, new producers, and new consumer groups?
- Can you characterize the dynamics of "sales" of your product based on its expected life cycle?
- Do you know which unit types will become more important, retain the same or lose their value on the market in the next three years?
- Do you have a clear picture, based on reliable information, about new promising market changes that will later favor you?
- Can you name the price at which tenants will agree to consistently rent your products, regardless of competitors?

By honest answering these questions, having analyzed for this purpose all the information available to you. You will be able to convince a potential investor of the seriousness of your intentions and the prospects of the proposed business.

In summary...

Briefly outline the goals you will strive for in your business for the next three years and the overall strategy for achieving them.

Chapter Ten: Competitors

Do you have competitors? What do you know about them? There are competitors in any business. Experienced people understand that there are always many competitors in the struggle for consumer money. However, newcomers to the real estate business tend to underestimate competitors and their influence on the course of their business.

One of the biggest mistakes you can make in a real estate business plan is to write, "We have no competitors." A knowledgeable, experienced investor will undoubtedly ignore a real estate business plan with such a statement for two reasons: 1) you have not fully studied all the conditions (realities) of your business; or 2) there is no market for your product (service), in other words, nobody needs them.

Do not be afraid of competitors, but, on the other hand, do not allow yourself to underestimate them. Don't let your emotions dictate your competitive decisions. Never overestimate the successes and failures, both your own and those of your competitors.

Respect for competitors will help you better understand your product or service and enable investors to realistically assess the strength of your company. This will allow you to learn how to better position your product in the market and in the eyes of consumers and it will help you identify all the favorable opportunities for your product.

Learn from your competitors. The basis of successful competition is the response to consumer requests, and studying your competitors will help you to know better what consumers want. Visit and study thriving rentals. Analyze their strengths and weaknesses. Buy from your competitor's ideas and improve on them.

When making competition decisions, keep in mind that you should only evaluate competitors who are in the same target market as you. If you are the owner of a high-end duplex in the city center, you should not consider the condominium next door as your competitor: you are not competing for the same customer at the same time.

It is tempting to assess your competitiveness based on the assertion that future consumers will prefer your units instead of competitors' own, and money will flow to you. Unfortunately, many other factors will determine your success in competing with other realtors and real estate business people. For example, a well-known realtor's name that inspires consumer confidence; or greater affordability of apartments; or a more perfect (even clever) system of selling them. All components of consumer preferences, including price, extra services, and location, should be taken into account when analyzing your competitiveness.

Be sure to remember that you must also consider negative factors. For example, if your target market is only interested in "prestigious" products, setting a low, affordable price would be a mistake and lead to a loss of competitive position.

Questions to ask yourself

So, the purpose of writing this section of the real estate business plan is to inform potential partners and investors about the difficulties of the upcoming competition in the market where your property(ies) would be located. When reading the material presented here, investors and partners should receive answers to the following questions:

- How are the competitors doing (rent volume, profitability, the introduction of new apartment models, extra service when it comes to dorms and hostels)?
- Do your competitors pay a lot of attention and money to advertising their units?
- What are their products: basic characteristics, quality level, design, customer opinion?
- What is the price level for competitors' products? What is their pricing policy, at least in general terms?
- Where do you see the strengths and weaknesses of your competitors?
- What are your potential competitors in the future?

The most important principle of the capital market is very simple - the more risky the investment, the more expensive it costs the borrower. Therefore, it is better to assess competitors soberly. But not to be afraid of them, but to indicate those gaps in their strategy or quality characteristics of products that open up a real chance to achieve success. Then the respect of investors and a higher chance of receiving funds are guaranteed.

Of course, you will not be able to give answers to all the questions formulated here. But try to get as much information as possible. The realism of your forecasts will depend on this, and the investor will feel that he is dealing with a serious person. If possible, try to analyze the market in terms of the competitiveness of your proposed housing units and make appropriate decisions.

Your marketing strategy

The future "health" of your business to an exceptional degree depends on your clarity of understanding of the current market situation and its possible development. The choices you make in marketing strategy will largely determine all other components of your business. That is why you must try to devote as much time as possible to this issue when preparing your real estate business plan.

We advise you to highlight and consider in detail the following components of a marketing strategy:

- Choice of markets: Determine which markets you want to penetrate.
- Entry policy: Name what kinds of housing or apartment units you want to offer to the market.
- Awareness: Describe the awareness channels you intend to use to bring your product to market. Will you advertise on your own or through third-party organizations?
- Sales plan: Describe how you will manage the marketing of your units and the promotion methods you intend to apply. What are the planned sales methods?
- Occupancy rate: Determine the occupancy rate that you plan to achieve for each housing unit in each market and what methods you will use to achieve sales growth. By expanding sales marketers or by looking for new forms of attracting customers?
- Profitability level: What is the level of profitability that you want to

achieve, or that you need (in other words, what is the maximum required and the desired size of profitability)?

- Advertising: How advertising will be organized and how much money are you going to allocate for it?
- Service: How services will be organized (e.g for hostels), how much will it cost, and will such a service be profitable?
- Public relations: How will you achieve a good reputation for yourself in the eyes of the public?
- Price policy: Describe the price level in each of the possible markets.

As you work on this section of your real estate business plan, consider the following questions. Try to provide answers to them. These questions will help you move in the right direction when developing your marketing strategy and prevent you from making rash decisions.

Many investors (and we remember that a real estate business plan is a document "for sale") consider this section of the real estate business plan as the most important. And this is natural: investors understand that the most excellent idea can fail because of a bad executor. Conversely, a good manager can "save" even a mediocre plan.

Describe your organization (existing or future) and the prospects for its development in the coming years. Your management team is one of the highlights. Indicate what kind of specialists (profile, education, work experience, salary level) are needed for a successful business. And prove that the candidates you proposed meet the specified requirements and have all the necessary qualities for a successful business.

Attach to the real estate business plan short biographies (1-2 pages) of the proposed specialists, do not forget to include their addresses and phone numbers here to provide the investor with a possibility to contact them. Indicate whether you are going to use the named specialists in the permanent staff or involve them in combination (as external experts, consultants, advertisers). If you have not yet found possible candidates for these positions, please include in the proposal where you are going to look for them, and is it possible to use the services of special organizations for the hiring of such professionals? However, remember that vacancies in the management team are a big flaw in your real estate business plan.

In the same section, it is necessary to give the organizational structure of your enterprise, which will clearly show: who will do what and when, the scheme of interaction of all services with each other, coordination and control of their activities. It is advisable in this section to discuss the issues of remuneration of management personnel, the relationship between the level of wages, and the results of production activities.

List the people you intend to include (or who are already on) the Board of Directors. Try not to include your relatives. Investors prefer to see a small team, which includes already well-proven businessmen/women associated with the field of activity of your company. Be sure to indicate how often the Board of Directors should meet and whether the directors have financial obligations to your company.

In the same section, name the total number of employees in your company, and how this number relates to the number of products you intend to manage.

Do not forget to form the relationship of management. And don't forget that the owner of a company is not always the best manager. Be sure to think over and describe the system of hiring workers and employees for your company. Who will do this? Is there a special service or person? Would your hiring policy be able to ensure that the right specialist is available for the required job at the right time? And will they understand the working principle of wage differentiation applied in your company? Have you prepared a written description of professional duties, requirements for the quality of their performance so that your employees know what and how to successfully complete the assigned work?

Think about the system of professional development for your employees. Remember! There should be no lackluster attitudes when working with staff!

In summary...

- Newcomers to the real estate business tend to underestimate competitors and their influence on the course of their business.
- If you have not yet found possible candidates for important positions,

include in the proposal where you are going to look for them, and whether it is possible to use the services of special organizations for the hiring of such professionals.

Chapter Eleven: Finding Investors and Closing the Deal

How to find an investor for your real estate company? As a business creator, you may have embarked on this great adventure on your own with your own funds. You now have desires for greatness. Know that you are not alone in this adventure. Indeed, you can benefit from a little help. Call on an investor! Indeed, appealing to investors is an excellent idea insofar as you will receive real support in your project.

The possibility is often offered to shareholders to set the conditions for collective decision-making. Thus, there is control as to the flow of associates, that is to say, that the entry of a new associate into the company or its refusal is decided collectively. A clause for this will be provided for in the company's articles of association.

The business plan, the key element of your financing request

It is at this stage that your charisma and professionalism must emerge. You have to show that you are a reliable and trusted business owner. As noted in Chapter 8, your plan must be solid. The business plan is the roadmap of your company. You detail the path you want to take and your needs to get there. This document transcribes the viability and relevance of your project. Any investor, upon reading this business plan, must be convinced of the viability of your project. Your development plan must be clear.

A business plan is therefore composed as follows:

- A complete market study
- The adopted business strategy
- The financial plan (legal obligation)

Maintain power in the face of a new investor

The arrival of a new investor should not mean a loss of power in your company. You have to, however, be particularly vigilant so as not to upset the balance of the partners. You must maintain control of your business despite the arrival of a new investor. Convince the investor(s) that you are a professional and be in charge of most of the decision-making. You can do this by convincing them with your winning business plan. In any case, there are a number of investment options to choose from, which I shall discuss below:

Business Angels: private investors

These investors will help you during the start-up phase in exchange for a percentage of your business. They finance companies with high potential. In addition, they bring their experience and expertise in their existing businesses to the table. Usually, very wealthy business angels are very involved in society, so you have to know how to accept and manage this interference if you have major projects.

As part of the search for private funds, you can open the capital of your company to individual investors by contacting Business Angels. Business Angels are private investors and generally successful entrepreneurs. Some are ready to invest under the impulse of a crush on your project. They however must be convinced of the gains and benefits that your business can generate and bring to them. We must not forget that a private investor is looking for an opportunity: he can invest from the start of the creation of your real estate company, or support the acceleration of activity in its market.

You must therefore contact Business Angels who have a certain affinity with the sector in which you operate or plan to operate in. It is, therefore, necessary to think carefully with whom to associate and to define the respective interests of each one.

Crowdfunding: find private investors quickly

The procedure of crowdfunding is very simple, just create a page call to donations or funding by explaining the project so clearly and attractively. You must indicate the duration of the fundraising and the desired amount. Then, professionals and individuals can choose to invest or not in the project.

Love Money: find money from individuals

The term Love Money refers to money that an entrepreneur will look for in his inner circle: family, friends, or even individuals that trust him/her. They are often the first people to turn to to find investors: those close to you are more inclined to trust you, to give you a helping hand to get started.

These people ask you to explain your project, the reasons for its success and must also be reassured of your ability to control the rudder before giving you any money. It is also an excellent training ground to present your pitch and argue with benevolent people before addressing investors who are more difficult to convince.

As a moral principle, it is important to warn your loved ones there is a small element of failure because their money can be lost: an excellent reason to "concrete" your project, by starting your business plan.

Enter a competition to win funds

Some project leaders or business creators participate in competitions, seduce the jury, and are allocated a budget to develop their company. The advantages of such competitions:

- be able to earn money without being accountable to anyone
- make yourself known as such competitions usually aired on TV, developing the image of your future company
- provides excellent training to gain confidence in presenting your pitch

The disadvantages of such competitions include:

- the amount collected is often not enough to sustain a project most of the time, it represents more of a boost
- not all competitions are open to any type of project and the selection process is tough

Check if the game is worth the effort before entering a contest and ask yourself the simple question: what will I win? In any case, if you do join and are not the big winner, it is always useful to learn from your participation and give better visibility to your project.

Ask for financial assistance from dedicated government organizations

Government organizations managed by your region, by the State, or even by the country you reside in may have implemented financial aid and subsidy schemes that are granted to business creators without request for reimbursement. It is therefore an avenue to be studied closely. However, care must be taken to respect the criteria defined by these organizations:

- the obligation to practice in a specific territory
- the obligation to develop an activity in a specific sector
- the obligation to fulfill all the legal conditions inherent to the business creator

Go to private equity firms

These private companies have the capacity to unlock very substantial private equity funds, up to millions of dollars.

When they invest in your company, they, therefore, acquire shares in your company. The main objective of these private investors is to realize a capital gain by selling their shares, which will have increased in value, most of the time in a maximum of 5 years.

Private equity firms therefore only invest in projects with high development potential. They are very demanding on the selection criteria, the financial results obtained, and ask to be informed regularly.

Private equity funds can be obtained:

- In the form of risk capital in the early stage: the investor takes a high risk because you are starting your activity and you have not yet imposed your offer on the market. The funds must allow you to finance and launch your project.
- In the form of development capital: the investor supports an already profitable business. The funds collected are then intended to support the growth of the company to finance a development on a larger scale, such as diversifying the offer of products or services, increasing the number of apartments, etc.

This environment has specific rules and codes: it is strongly recommended to be accompanied by a lawyer before contacting these private investors.

Apply for an honor loan

An honor loan is granted to the business creator or a buyer: the borrower undertakes to repay this loan over a period of 2 to 5 years. The loan of honor is a personal loan: it is therefore to the manager who is granted the loan of honor, and not to his company.

The advantages of the loan of honor:

- A zero rate, you pay no interest
- It facilitates the granting of a bank loan
- It is granted by a committee bringing together entrepreneurs, bankers, accountants, which testifies to the seriousness of your project if you get the loan
- You do not have to present any guarantees or personal surety
- For 1 dollar of honorary loan granted, you can obtain on average 8 dollars of additional loan from a bank

Most of the time, the loan of honor is granted on condition of subscribing to a bank loan in addition. It is often available to college undergraduates or fresh college graduates.

Negotiate a loan with a bank

Banks help entrepreneurs finance their projects: in return for the credit they grant, they get paid with interest that must also be repaid. Before contacting a bank, it is advisable to meet the best conditions to obtain your bank loan - provide personal guarantees.

Banks are the private investors who take the least risk if any at all. A banker will gladly tell you that you don't finance a business like you finance a car. The wise entrepreneur will approach the bank with a solid financial record: he must make the bank understand that it is lucky that the manager asks him for a bank loan, and not the other way around ...

Other forms of financing

Venture capital is a type of investment that supports development efforts. The fundraiser helps finance the entrepreneur's needs. Venture capital companies are specialized in long-term investment. They also provide strategic input, with their knowledge of the market. They are of considerable help to young leaders.

Investment funds are also another type of investment that could support your real estate business. They invest directly by taking a stake in the capital, hence they become owners in your business. Here again, it will be necessary to be able to present an attractive project, in order to seduce them and convince them to invest in your project.

Be well prepared before taking action

As you most likely understand now, first of all, writing your business plan is essential. It must include all the arguments and quantified elements that demonstrate the viability and potential of your project:

- The state of your market and why it is promising
- Studying the competition in your market
- Your promise, how you differentiate yourself from the competition
- Obstacles in your way
- Your resource strategy, with a precise action plan
- Your assets, represented by your team, your associates, your technology, etc.
- Your sales forecast
- Your financial forecast, your cash flow
- The growth curve you envision

If the numbers speak for themselves, the "shape" of your business plan also matters: it reveals the intelligence, wit, and liveliness of the leader, the pilot at the controls of a rocket that must take off to reach the moon.

Secondly, you have to know how to put yourself in the shoes of an investor and ask yourself the following questions:

- Who is this person really, is he a sweet talker or someone who has thought through his project? Is the management operational?
- Is this project reliable? Does it involve risks? What kind?
- Have I ever seen similar cases with successes or failures?
- Is this project piloted by the right team?
- What is the return on investment? How much will it earn me?

Third, keep in mind that you should not sell the skin of the bear before killing it: you have to know how to keep your head on your shoulders and evaluate lower forecasts, rather than fall from very high in the event of a fateful moment.

Another common mistake made by entrepreneurs is to ignore or forget about marketing expenses, which are essential to business development. We must anticipate this load and consider it as an investment which must bring/attract customers to our properties to ensure a constant turnover.

You now have all the keys to fundraising. Have a desire for greatness and call on investors to carry out your project!

In summary…

- As part of the search for funds, you can open up the capital aspect of your company to individual investors by contacting Business Angels, among others.
- Be well prepared before taking action as writing your business plan is essential.

Chapter Twelve: Getting Off the Ground - Key Roles, Capital Distribution and Profit Splitting

Not a week goes by without me being asked how to divide the potential profits of a real estate project with partners. Here is something to feed your thinking on this subject. Note that there is no standard scenario. Everything is based on negotiation and the relationship between the parties.

How to distribute the capital of a real estate company between its founders/investors?

The question of the distribution of the initial capital must be approached before the creation of the company - and in consultation with all the founding partners. Below, I offer you a general overview of the main issues related to the distribution of capital - in particular in the context of a real estate business startup.

1. Choose the right number of founding partners

Even before the question of the methods of distribution of capital among the investors, there is that of the number of investors. What is the ideal number of partners to create a startup? We can distinguish three possibilities:

Only one founding partner - This formula has at least one advantage: it de facto eliminates the question of the distribution of the company's capital. But in reality, going alone on a startup-type entrepreneurial project is difficult to maintain. For at least three reasons:

a. the entire workload rests on the same person,

b. the development of a project requires the combination of several skills that are rarely found in a single individual and,

c. in the absence of an interlocutor with whom to exchange on an equal footing, it is more difficult to take a step back when things get complicated or do not go as planned. The vast majority of startups are founded by at least two partners.

Two and four partners - The optimal formula is undoubtedly to be found within this range. This makes it possible both to play on the complementarity of skills and networks and to avoid an excessive dispersion of capital and decision-making power.

Five or more partners - A priori, that's too much…. Either there is no assumed leader, or the team does not know what should be (and not be) a founding partner. Either way, there is a problem.

To understand the issues and choose the right number of founders, you have to be perfectly clear about the role of the founder. A founder is more than just a contributor. There is a difference in nature between the two, which stems from a very different level of engagement. It is important to distinguish between the two:

A founder is a person who invests his body and soul in the project, who lives for it. He generally devotes all his professional time to it - quits his job if he was an employee - and undertakes to become involved in the long term in the development of the project. He is ready to make a lot of sacrifices, and in particular not to pay himself a salary until he has succeeded in raising funds. He knows that his project involves a risk, but nevertheless embarks on the adventure out of conviction and ambition.

A contributor is a person who engages in the project alongside his main professional activity. He invests part of his time (which may vary) in the project, but never all of his time. He does not necessarily have the soul of an entrepreneur, nor the taste for risk. The "emotional" link he maintains with the project is more tenuous. The contributor is in no way ready to sacrifice himself (sacrificing his time, his weekends, his savings) in the success of the project - except in a pinch if he anticipates substantial and certain prospects of gain.

Founders must also be distinguished from employees. An employee is ready to devote all his time to the development of the project but on the condition of being paid. It is important to make these distinctions. It is in the founders that investors invest. It is the skills, motivation, and complementarity of the founders that base the decision of investors. For a simple reason: it is only on the founders that the success or failure of the project rests.

The number of founders will have a logical influence on the distribution of capital. The more founders there are, the more the capital is diluted. On the other hand, the number of investors does not presume the egalitarian or unequal nature of the distribution of capital. We will discuss this later in this chapter.

2. Guarantee the credibility and investment of the founding partners

A founding partner with a share of less than 10% or 15% of the share capital will appear less credible to investors. This sends the wrong signal to investors. You have to get into their heads: investors will tend to perceive these very minority founders as partners who should not be.

Beyond this issue of perception and credibility vis-à-vis investors, a founder who has too low a percentage of shares will be deemed to have little weight internally when important or difficult decisions have to be taken. Few shares = little decision-making power. It is the cohesion between the founders - which is based on mutual listening and a certain form of equality in the relationship - which is at stake here. After a while, he will tend to consider that he is not being remunerated at the fair value of his contribution, generating spite and frustration, or will end up becoming a real "stowaway".

In summary, we must avoid a founder having too little invested capital, because this has an impact on his credibility with third parties, but also on the cohesion of the founding team.

In the context of a real estate startup, the distribution of shareholding percentages could also be set based on concrete but non-financial contributions. This includes first and foremost the degree of involvement of the founder, their experience, their skills, their credibility, their role in the genesis of the project, etc. In short, it must be set before approaching investors. If a partner brings a lot more financially than the others, his contribution can be considered as internal fundraising, with the application of an issue premium to be negotiated between the different founders. If one of the founders is broke and cannot invest the money that corresponds to his share in the distribution of capital, he gets slightly less after profits are split.

3. Promote an unequal distribution of roles

A startup must have a true decision-maker leader, with the power to decide when a difficult decision needs to be made. Without leadership, the startup is exposed to the status quo, to hesitation in decision-making, to soft consensus, to immobility, lack of responsiveness, slowness of execution. However, remember that the key to a startup's success lies in the execution of the project much more than in the initial idea.

Only an unequal distribution of capital makes this leadership possible. Unless you have two very talented founders, with an equivalent level of skills and experience - which is very rare and not necessarily desirable. The unequal distribution of roles also reflects a reality that can be observed in all startups: the contribution of the founders is never equal. Some bring more, even a lot more to the project than others. From a certain point of view, the inequality in the distribution of the roles of the company is - contrary to what one might think - the fairest choice, the most equitable. It would be equality that would be unfair.

Yes, some will argue that an equal distribution promotes team cohesion, solidarity, and trust between the founders. However, the people who chose egalitarian distribution often end up regretting it as a posteriori. All of this brings us to the next point.

4. Define a coherent grid of criteria to distribute the roles

When the company is created, the capital must be distributed rationally and equitably between the founders. How to avoid endless discussions loaded with effects which do not advance the business project? Answer: by applying a capital allocation framework! The objective of a framework is to allow you to distribute your capital according to objective criteria.

The downside is that these frameworks do not necessarily take into account the specificities of each project. For example, from one project to another, technical skills can play a more or less important role. The distribution criteria and their weighting must be adapted to each project so that the distribution of capital is the most consistent. The ideal is therefore to build a custom framework yourself. How? or What? It's quite simple:

- You start by listing all the elements that you want to promote, which correspond to the different contributions in the project (for example, the contribution to the initial idea), or areas of actions/skills necessary for the success of the project in the first one or two years (for example mastery of investor negotiations, business plan writing, for the creation of the building plan drawing skill, etc.).

- You then assign an importance coefficient to each criterion retained (the coefficients must be validated by all the founders).
- Finally, you distribute the points between the partners on each criterion. For example, on the criterion of contribution to the idea of the project: 30% for founder X, 70% for founder Y, and 0% for founder Z.

To help you in creating your own framework, here is a list of possible criteria:

- Starting idea. Who had the initial idea for the project? It is quite consistent that the founder behind the idea receives a capital bonus. Which coefficient to choose? This question can only be answered on a case-by-case basis. If the idea is really revolutionary, it seems logical to assign a large coefficient to this criterion.
- Validation of the idea (transformation of the initial idea into a structured project). We can imagine different criteria corresponding to the different actions for the validation of the idea: design of the business plan, supervision of the market study, meetings with professionals of the sector, benchmark, technical model, operational prototype, etc.
- Who is/will be the CEO? The CEO receives a capital bonus because he plays a more important role than the other founders.
- Time invested: founders who work full time earn more points than those who work part-time. If everyone works full time (as is often the case), those who work more (on weekends for example) should receive more points.
- Skill levels in the various relevant fields: technical development, marketing, design, commercial, legal, administrative. We measure here the skill level of the founders but also the degree of investment of each. For certain fields, in particular technical fields, the degree of investment is directly linked to the level of skills. But in most cases, it's about assessing individual roles rather than skill level. For example: who will take care of the legal and administrative aspects? If it is founder 3, it makes sense to give him a capital bonus.
- Level of experience in other professional contexts, notably in project

management. Entrepreneurs are more and more efficient in their projects. It is quite logical that serial entrepreneur founders receive a capital bonus.

- The size of the network of potential investors. The founder who collects the most investments thanks to his network must obtain more points. We can also take as a criterion the size of everyone's network in general.

Obviously, you are free to add other criteria, delete some that do not seem relevant to you, or create sub-criteria. The most important thing is to take the time to choose the criteria and the coefficients allowing them to be weighted. These choices must be concerted among all the founders. You should aim for objectivity as much as possible.

5. Option planning as an adjustment mechanism

The distribution of the share capital is not fixed. It is called upon to evolve, with the arrival of new associate investors along the way, and the possible departure of certain associates. The implementation of an option plan makes it possible to resolve the problems of alignment of interests over time, to define the conditions adjusting the distribution and consolidation of the capital over time. In the case of a real estate startup, changes most often occur at the time of the arrival of a new investor, following the completion of a fundraising. Moreover, in many cases, the investor wants to become the majority partner.

There is a certain practice that allows the founders to retain decision-making power and avoid the dilution of the company's role management system. This involves the creation of different class actions - the founders have an absolute interest in ensuring that investors' shares do not lead to the granting of any decision-making power. It is possible to offer investors priority dividend shares that do not give the right to any voting rights. It is also possible to issue what are called investment certificates, which are securities distinct from shares that grant their beneficiary pecuniary rights (right of information for example), but no voting rights.

I hope to have shed some light on this complex and delicate issue. One thing is certain: the way in which you organize the distribution of the initial roles and capital will partly determine the success of your entrepreneurial project. The issue must be taken seriously so that you get off to a good start.

Who gets their hands on a windfall?

Contrary to what most people think, the most difficult thing in real estate is not to find financing, but to find a good bargain. Believe me, it is much easier to find someone willing to invest with you than to find a motivated seller who will agree to sell his building at a discount or a building with high untapped potential.

If you are the one on the team that brings the other parties the windfall in question, you have some bargaining power. You can decide to do the project with whoever you want unless of course, you have previously planned that you will invest with such or such a person if you get your hands on a good deal.

Who will take care of the project?

In flip selling mode, who will do the work and/or manage the work? One of the partners or even a third person? The time invested is to be taken into consideration because this portion is often overwhelming. While this person will see to the good progress of the work, he will not do anything else and will have to be paid accordingly. Either by immediate income or by an additional percentage of profit sharing.

When you own buildings for the long term, you also have to ask yourself these questions: who will take care of the day-to-day management of the building and administration? Will you hire someone to do it or divide these tasks between yourselves? And in this case, good coordination will be required and the distribution of tasks will have to be clearly defined between the partners.

Who will guarantee the loan?

Finding the bargain and injecting cash are two essential aspects to consider in your projects. But who will be the one who can finance the building and who will stand surety against the creditor? Who will be able to go to the bank for financing, if any? If none of them qualify with a bank, you should consider using a private lender to finance your project. But beware! In such a case, make sure you have a quick repayment plan if the interest on the private loan is high. Otherwise, you could be ruined if the project deadlines get longer.

If you invest with one or more partners, I invite you to have a good agreement to govern your relations, whether it is a shareholders' agreement, a partnership agreement, or an indivision agreement, depending on whether you are buying through a joint-stock company, a general partnership or between co-owners.

This agreement will allow, among other things, to provide for the mechanisms in the event of the death of a partner, a conflict, or the withdrawal of one of the partners, including you. What percentage of interest will be paid to those who inject the liquidity? Sometimes, we include a division of tasks and responsibilities, but we must be careful not to design a framework that is too rigid. You have to keep a little flexibility since everyone's role often changes over time.

Above all, do not try to write this agreement yourself to save a few hundred dollars! Call in the professionals. In addition, take the time to fully understand it and sign it once it is drafted. I've seen too many people who have unsigned shareholder agreements who have argued afterward.

It is difficult to get along when the bickering breaks out. Sign it and enforce it when the time comes. If the partners have fully understood their rights and obligations, discussions will be easier in the future.

Get involved!

What could be worse than partners who express the desire to invest with you and who, once the bargain has been found, withdraw under the pretext of being associated with another project? To avoid this unfortunate situation, have a subscription agreement (in the case of an investment by a joint-stock company) or a letter of agreement (in other cases) which will provide you with some protection in this regard. Again, consult a lawyer who will be able to properly draft this agreement.

Psychometric test

You read that right. Before embarking on a real estate adventure with another first-timer, wouldn't it be wise to make sure you have a minimum of compatibility? There is a multitude of products and services on the market in this regard. Several people have used the evaluation offered by Atmanco for free. Visit the site for more details.

In conclusion, I invite you to always keep in mind that your association should remain a win-win situation. Nothing is worse than when one of the partners feels wronged. You can do it!

In summary...

- A founder is a person who invests body and soul in the project, who lives for it.
- They generally devote all their professional time to it - quit their job, and undertake to become involved in the long term in the development of the project.

Chapter Thirteen: Putting Pen to Paper

Business people are divided into those who like to work with numbers and those who are afraid of them. For those in the first category, this section of the real estate business plan is undoubtedly the most interesting. If you consider yourself to be in the second category, you may be intimidated by the number of forms that need to be filled out to develop this section. However, this must be done.

Financial plan

This section of the real estate business is intended to summarize the previous materials and present them digitally, or rather in value terms. There is nothing magical, or even more dangerous than numbers. They simply reflect the decisions that you have made in the previous sections. If you decide to advertise your apartments and homes weekly in a local newspaper, your financial plan should include a figure that reflects this decision. If you want to rent some units at reduced prices, the corresponding figure will reflect this in the real estate business plan.

Every business decision comes with a number and taken together, these numbers form the backbone of your financial plan. These numbers cannot be taken simply "from the ceiling", because all financial forms are interconnected and one mistake gives rise to another. Therefore, your numbers should always be the result of careful calculations.

Even if you are not able to prepare the financial statements yourself, you must be able to read and analyze them. Only then can you successfully run a company. Make it a habit to read your company's financial statements on a monthly basis. Don't wait for your accountant to report. Check rental and sales information regularly. You will feel more confident making decisions based on this financial information. Never associate your business decisions with mood. All decisions must be based on financial information. Be sure to take "lessons" from a professional accountant who will explain to you all the financial terms and teach you how to read a financial statement.

It can be recommended to use computer accounting programs such as

Gnumeric, Excel, or Quattro Pro for drawing up a financial plan and in further work. These programs are widely available and convenient for people with average business experience and computer skills. For novices, the Microsoft Excel program is more suitable.

Types of financial forms

The financial section of a real estate business plan should contain the three most important forms:

- Gains and losses report (In our practice, this report is called "Statement of financial results and their use")
- Cash flow statement
- Enterprise balance

Gains and losses report

Usually, investors want to see a projected financial performance for three or even five years ahead (for new companies), and for existing ones, in addition, for the past three or five years.

The profit and loss statement shows whether your company will receive (or, for an operating company, whether it is already receiving) profit, that is, the level of profitability of your company, how much money you will have after all the expenses incurred. However, this report does not reflect the total "value" of your company, nor how much cash it has. The company may start to lose money, which will be reflected in the same report, however, its value may still be large enough, or the company may be profitable, but not have enough cash to pay the bills (due to cash flow problems).

This report should be read from top to bottom. The top line shows the total sales. The second is the included value-added tax (VAT). The following lines show the expenses incurred. The difference between the volume of sales (net of VAT) and costs shows the balance sheet profit. The sum of profit and accrued wages is taxable income. The last line of the income statement is the income remaining at the disposal of the firm. If the company's expenses exceed revenues, in the last line of the income statement there will be a negative number. In accounting practice, the minus sign "-" is replaced by brackets ().

Cash flow statement

This shows if the company has (or will) have the cash to pay the bills. This report is one of the most important financial documents. And although in our accounting practice it is not currently mandatory, you cannot do without it when drawing up a real estate business plan. After all, if you cannot pay your workers and employees, pay suppliers' bills. You will not be able to run the business for a long time and you, of course, will not be able to sleep at night.

The cash flow statement does not represent your profit. It only shows how much money you have in the bank, how much cash "comes" in and out of the account in each month of the year.

When developing this form, show separately the cash that you will receive from the sale/rentals of your units and from other activities (for example, financial transactions, interest paid to you by the bank, receiving investments). This will give you a clear picture of the sources of your cash and show you the possibility of investing in newer properties or holding on for a bit.

Enterprise balance

The enterprise balance shows how much your company is worth. For newbies in the business, this is the least understood form. This balance sheet provides a "snapshot" of your company's value. It shows the value of all its components (land, buildings, furniture, equipment, inventories). It also shows the size of all liabilities (loans received, share capital, settlements with creditors, salaries for company employees, etc.).

The difference between the assets of the enterprise and the long- and short-term liabilities of the company shows your business net worth. There is a total for a section of the enterprise balance sheet that displays "Sources of equity and equivalent funds." "Asset" and "liability" are always equal. That is why this document is called "Balance".

To prepare the "Balance", be sure to involve a professional accountant, especially for calculating such indicators. However, remember that you must understand the meanings of all indicators and be able to "read" the balance sheet.

The financial plan also contains the calculation of the break-even point of business.

Investment program

This section should outline a plan for obtaining funds to create or expand your real estate business enterprise. The first question is: how much money is needed in general for the implementation of this project? The second question: where do you plan to receive this money, in what form? And the third question: when can we expect a full return of the funds received and investors receive income from them?

When attracting credit funds to finance your project, do not forget about the possibility of obtaining not only a bank, but also a privately-sourced loan, which can be provided on much more favorable terms (for example, by participants in the project in question, or by angel investors).

Environmental protection

In modern conditions, characterized by a rapid deterioration of the environmental situation, a decrease in natural resources, uncontrolled population growth, the accumulation of stress factors, the concept of social and ethical marketing is increasingly being put into the basis of the company's activities.

When this notion is implemented, the corporation assumes a high level of responsibility, not only toward individual clients (buyers or renters) but also toward society and its future, providing a high standard of living while also maintaining a high level of quality. Notably, the creation of the notion of social and ethical marketing is closely related to the efforts of consumer organizations to safeguard their interests as well as the efforts of environmentally conscious organizations.

Consumers are influenced by them to re-evaluate many of their needs from the perspective of protecting personal and public interests (health, environment, ecology), which leads to a shift in the concept of commercial activities of many companies, as well as their appeal to the concept of social and ethical marketing as a result. This means that for this notion to be implemented, all members of society must demonstrate a certain level of "maturity," as described above.

Your real estate business plan should reflect your social maturity. Consider the potential environmental impact of your building operations, both now and in the future. In what manner the trash will be disposed of, if they can be further processed, and whether or not there will be problems with the disposal of packing materials are all important considerations (bags, bottles, cans, boxes, etc.). Will you have a "green" space within your apartments? A few flowers, maybe? Describe your plans to mitigate any potential detrimental impact on the environment, as well as the directions and timelines for implementing these measures. Are you planning to use this action of your organization to promote your brand in an advertising campaign? After all, your care for the general public's welfare can help you to establish a positive reputation and attract new customers.

In summary...

- The financial section of a real estate business plan is very important.
- Your real estate business plan should reflect your social maturity.
- Consider the potential environmental impact of your building operations, both now and in the future.

Chapter Fourteen: Risk Assessment and Insurance

The concept of risk, its assessment, forecasting, and even its management is the content of this concluding chapter. Answer the question: how to reduce risks and losses? The answer should consist of two parts, the first of which specifies organizational measures to prevent risks, and the second - the risk insurance program.

Risk assessment is one of the most difficult and least accurate elements of financial analysis. It will be necessary to determine as accurately as possible all unforeseen occurrences/circumstances that may arise in the future. Traditionally considered are the following factors:

1. **Market risk:**
   - Will there be a market in the future?
   - Will the market grow at a rate that will help your business?
   - Is your gross margin sufficient to withstand a price war, if any?

2. **Risk of competing buildings:**
   - Will your competitors be able to develop newer buildings that will make yours obsolete?
   - Can any new structures prevent the enterprise from successfully fulfilling its plans?

3. **Risk of completion or technical risk:**
   - Is the proposed project or subject of activity reliable enough for everything to work as planned?

4. **External risk:**
   - What is the likelihood that someone or something (government, trade unions, subcontractors, transport, etc.) will stop or slow down the operation of the enterprise? Do you have any suggestions for solving these problems?

5. Internal risk:

- Do you have enough personnel for the enterprise to function normally?
- If not, is it possible to get it on time and on favorable terms?

6. Political risk:

- Is there, or is it expected, any government regulation that could hinder your success?
- Will mandatory permits from special authorities, for example, environmental protection, building authorities, etc., be obtained, when required?

7. Resource risk:

- Will there be a sufficient number of customers, buyers, or renters for a period significantly longer than the maturity of financial resources costs?
- Do the partners have enough financial, human, and intellectual resources to complete the planned project?

8. Capital investment risk:

- Will inflation, changes in exchange rates, or government policies significantly affect the volume of investments?
- What is the probability that as a result of these changes you will completely or partially lose your capital?

A real program of "risk management" should be developed based on a study of the specifics of the real estate business branch you choose and the intricacies of the insurance market.

When developing a business loss protection program, attention is usually focused on the following three areas:

1. Risk of loss of property - exposure of your property, including real and "invisible" assets, to the risk of complete loss or damage (fire, theft).
2. Risk of loss of time - arises in connection with the possibility of

disruptions and interruptions in the functioning of your business or delays in receiving payments for investments made.

3. Default Risk - this includes your liability to customers, people in your business, to those who use or rely on your products or services, and to society in general.

The insurance business is based on an insurance policy

An insurance policy is a contract under which an insurance company (insurer) assumes the obligation to pay compensation (insurance premium) if any undesirable accidental event occurs that causes losses. In exchange for this service, you, for your part, undertake to pay certain amounts (insurance premiums) to the insurer.

The insurance policy indicates what type of risk it covers, in what time frame, and for what amount. The insurance policy may also indicate the procedure for carrying out the procedures related to the execution of the contract: how to draw up an insurance claim, how to terminate the contract, how to determine the amount of insurance remuneration due, and how to increase the amount of insurance coverage. Insurance policies can be specific or general.

A special policy establishes (describes) each item of the insured property, determines its volume and value (an inventory of the most expensive items from a set of equipment or a collection of works of art can serve as such an example). The general policy offers great flexibility in determining the amount of insurance compensation, setting only the value of the insured property as a whole. The amount of insurance compensation is not determined for each individual item from the composition of the insured property.

The package policy insures many possible risks in a single complex contract. When similar, similar types of risk are brought together and insured in a single "package", you can successfully avoid the overlap of the areas of coverage of different specific insurance policies. On the other hand, combining dissimilar risks in one policy can render you less flexible in purchasing other insurance policies and, moreover, make it difficult to compare competing insurance policies.

Risk insurance is provided through the following algorithm:

1. Determine the volume and structure of tangible assets that are at risk of loss or damage.
2. Highlight the risks that can be avoided by taking certain precautions, calculate your costs for the implementation of these measures.
3. Decide which type of insurance (general or special) can better protect you at a lower cost compared to the cost of taking precautions.
4. If the cost of insurance is only slightly less than the cost of organizing the precautions, consider whether it is worth wasting your time and money, is it not better to take precautions?

Follow these rules to prevent both underinsurance and over-insurance:

1. Clearly identify all types of your legal responsibility: for the performance of contracts, leases, supplies, and all other transactions - and take care of covering the risks arising from possible failure to fulfill these obligations.
2. Determine the likelihood of losing some sums of money for details not covered by the deal. Be aware of the non-operational risks associated, for example, with a broken bed in your rented-out rooms.
3. Assess the degree of dependence of your business on sudden interruptions in its functioning due to fire or plumbing-related accidents, or other disruptions.
4. Be aware of the risks associated with the safe operation and use of your units by buyers, renters, and even third parties. Such risks can also be insured.
5. When you have converted your estimates into a monetary equivalent, do not get lost, since you need to insure only a small amount of all the risks that you may face. Your insurance specialist will separate the risks that are insured from those that are not.
6. Once you have determined what can be profitably insured, forget about all the small risks that do not need to be covered. Small loss insurance is usually an expensive fad.
7. Finally, forget about risk insurance that you can handle yourself in some other way "at less cost and effort".
8. One more note. Don't let your risk reduction program end with the

purchase of an insurance policy. Even with insurance, losses mean inconvenience at best and ruin at worst. Preventing the possibility of loss is central to the risk mitigation program and the implementation of this program should not be limited to insurance itself.

In summary...

Answer the question: how to reduce risks and losses?

- Highlight the risks that can be avoided by taking certain precautions, calculate your costs for the implementation of these measures.
- If the cost of insurance is only slightly less than the cost of organizing the precautions, consider whether it is worth wasting your time and money, is it not better to take precautions?

Final Words

To do!

1. Involve all future leaders of your company in the process of developing your real estate business plan.
2. Make sure your real estate business plan is logical, clear, readable, and as short as possible.
3. Make your personal contribution to your future business by investing time and, if necessary, money in developing your real estate business plan. However, remember that a plan is not a business yet and that one gram of what was done is more valuable than a kilogram of what was planned!
4. Try in advance to find friends and investors who will bring money to your bank account, even if you have to postpone writing a real estate business plan.
5. Find out what your target investors (entrepreneur, bank, leasing company) really want and dislike, and develop your real estate business plan with this in mind.
6. Realistically estimate the possible sales/rental volumes and put them in based on the developed financial plan, and not vice versa. Do not wishful think!
7. Never describe a process using jargon or terminology that only a specialist can understand, as this will reduce the effectiveness of your real estate business plan. Nobody will invest in what they don't understand.
8. Don't consider a friendly handshake or verbal praise to be a positive outcome of the deal. The deal is considered complete when you receive your check!

And now about the "secrets".

1. There are no secrets to success. An understanding and practical mastery of the knowledge presented in this book, along with hard work, will bring results.
2. If there is a secret, there is always someone else besides you who

knows about it. Therefore, the search for secrets is a futile exercise.

3. The happiness of an entrepreneur is money in your bank account!
4. One year is enough to learn the theory part for others, but if you want to learn entrepreneurship (in other words, work for yourself), it will take a whole lifetime.
5. Don't spend more than you get!
6. Above all, your success is neither financial nor technical. Everything depends on you!

References

. Agnes (2000): Is Financial Services at the 'End of Geography'? Local Integration and Territorialization in the Interest Rate Swaps Industry, Economic Geography, 76, pp. 347–366.

V. Bailey, A. Kumar, and D. Ng, "Home Bias of US Individual Investors: Causes and Consequences, AFA 2007 meeting paper

. Baum, Managing Specific Risk in Property Portfolios, Property Research Institute, 2007.

Baum, A. (2008). Unlisted Property Funds: Capital for Developing Countries.

Commercial Real Estate Investment: A Strategic Approach, A. Baum, 2009.

Baum, A., and Crosby, N. (2008), Blackwell's Property Investment Appraisal (3e).

. Baum and C. Lizieri, Who Owns the City of London? Residential Real Estate Finance, pp. 87–100

. Baum and C.B. Murray, Understanding the Barriers to Real Estate Investment in Emerging Economies, 2010. Reading University's School of Real Estate and Working document for planning

. Bekaert, Market Integration and Investment Barriers in Emerging Equity, 1995.

World Bank Economic Review, 9, pp. 75–107.

. Bekaert and C. Harvey, 2002, Research in Emerging Markets Finance: A Look Back, Review of Emerging Markets, vol. 3, pp. 429–448.

International Capital Market Equilibrium with Investment Barriers, F. Black (1974).

Financial Economics Journal, vol. 1, no. 4, pp. 337–352.

. Eichengreen (2001): Capital Account Liberalization: What Do Cross-Country Comparisons Tell Us

A Model of International Asset Pricing, C.S. Eun and S. Janakiramanan, 1986

. Graham, C. Harvey, and H. Huang, Investor Competence, Trading Frequency, and Personal Prejudice, National Bureau of Economic Research Working Paper

Domestic and Foreign Bias in Real Estate, T. Imazeki and P. Gallimore, 2010

ournal of Real Estate Research, vol. 26, pp. 367–390.

. Lahiri, Foreign Direct Investment: An Overview of Issues, International Economic Review, 2009.

Economic and Financial Review, 18, 1, pp. 1–2.

ournal of Real Estate, Convergence Trends in European Real Estate Equities 23(1), 2003, pp. 1–23

. McAllister and C. Lizieri, Monetary Integration and Real Estate Markets, 2006

.P. Nishiotis (2004) Does Indirect Investment Barriers Affect Capital Markets?

Quinn, D., Inclan, C., and Toyoda, M. (2001): Capital Accounts: How and Where

. Razin, E. Sadka, and C.W. Yuen (1998): Capital Flows in a Pecking Order.

nternational Tax Principles, Journal of International Economics, vol. 44, no. 45, pp. 45–68.

. Reinhart and P. Montiel (1999): Do Capital Controls Affect the Volume and Quality of Capital?

Capital Flows: What Is Their Composition? MPRA Paper 13710, Evidence from the 1990s

.M. Stulz, A Model of International Asset Pricing, The Journal of Financial Economics, 1981.